Born to Rule

Robert Farrier

STM PUBLICATION

Lake City, FL

STM PUBLICATION

Unless otherwise indicated, all Scripture quotations are from *The Holy Bible, New King James Version.* © Copyright 1982

Scripture quotations noted NLT are taken from The New Living Translation, © Copyright 1996. All rights reserved. Used by permission.

Scripture quotations noted NCV are taken from The Holy Bible, New Century Version © Copyright 2005 by Thomas Nelson, Inc. Used by permission.

ISBN-13: 978-09789842-6-7
ISBN-10: 0978984269

For additional copies you can order from:
Publisher or online:
www.kingdomfaithconnection.com

Reference: 1. Inspirational. 2. Culture and Worldviews. 3. Kingdom Living

Special Acknowledgement

I would like to acknowledge the following people who helped make this book possible: The late Dr. Clarence E. Fast, Pastor and friend who first taught me how to be sensitive to the leading of the Spirit of God; and to Dr.'s Chad and Katie Bardsley, who having endured two teaching sessions of this material, inspired and encouraged the turning of my notes into the writing of this book.

In 1979, Professor James Jones, Southeastern University, introduced me to DeVern F. Fromke through his book, *The Ultimate Intention*. Although I did not understand fully what he was saying, I did not discard the material but put it in an imaginary shoebox and set it on a shelf. Fifteen years later, while reading the Word, the Holy Spirit brought back to my remembrance the message of this book. The message of God's Ultimate Intention was internalized and became the catalyst for some of the teaching found in this book regarding God's Grand Plan and the message of the internal cross that has been lost by the Church.

Three years ago I came across another writer, Dr. Myles Munroe, who has written, *Rediscovering the Kingdom*. My excitement was overwhelming as God's was confirming what I had been teaching for years. God does not entrust his revelation of what He is doing to just one man. He raises up his prophets from all over the world to bring this message forth in order that his people might hear what the Spirit is saying to the Church today.

I would also like to thank Paul Moore, STM Publications, for his tireless work in bringing this book to press.

May all glory and the honor been given to the One to whom this book is dedicated, King Jesus Christ.

Contents

Created by God. . .

Born to Rule

Preface

In this first book of a two-volume series, the author is presenting a means for preparedness for God's people to reign and rule with Christ in His Kingdom. However, to do so we must first be prepared to be an Overcomer in light of the pending chaos and horrendous trouble that is coming upon the earth. He is also providing insight into what is behind this mayhem that looms in the horizon.

This first volume is about Transformation while the second will deal with Empowerment. This material has been taught to those living in countries that would be considered the poorest in the world. But whether the people are Christian, Hindu, Muslim, or Buddhist the message is the same. The spiritual warfare that the people in these lands are experiencing, the people in the Western world, but especially the USA, will be going through in the years ahead.

What is fast approaching will affect every race on every continent. It will affect the rich and the poor, the educated and the illiterate, and the rulers as well as the slaves. That which is in front of us will bring monumental change.

The author wishes you to see a full-length feature film that starts before creation and goes straight to the conclusion, the end of this world. The plans have already been made and are now being carried out to tie the economies and the well-being of the world's nations together so that if one fails they all fail. To the natural man there seems to be only one solution that will prevent such a catastrophe; a new world order that has global governance.

It is not a man or a group of men that are parlaying their influence and money to create a New World Order, as one would assume. These powerful men, without knowing it, are mere pawns being played by the one who has more at stake in this game of life. His name is Satan. However, to Satan it is not a game because what is at stake is his kingdom. To rule the whole earth is his goal.

Whoever gets the kingdom gets something more valuable than property and things; whoever gets the kingdom receives WORSHIP from those who are subjects of the kingdom. The battleground is the culture of the kingdom. Whoever controls the culture gets to wear the crown of KING.

The Kingdom Culture that God instilled into Adam and Eve was the first target of Satan after their expulsion from the Garden of Eden. The family of Adam and Eve soon found themselves in kingdom war within their family. Cain murdered his brother Abel, and then left to form the first humanistic family of the world. Man then found himself under the first state government, where men were ruling over men instead of God ruling over men. Cain's family developed its own culture and the war continued.

While Satan has been leading humanity onward to the final Battle of Armageddon, thinking that this will bring about his great overthrow of God's Kingdom, Jesus Christ quietly announced that a New World Order has come. Jesus made the announcement, *"Repent, for the kingdom of Heaven is at hand."* This announcement is the fulfillment of the promise given to Adam and Eve. It proclaimed that at the conclusion of the ages, all kingdoms of the earth will come under the governmental authority of Jesus Christ and He will rule in Righteousness as King of kings and Lords of lords.

Leading up to this final battle, a number of dramatic events will be experienced in the earth. Many of these events are now being witnessed, such as changes in nature (increase in number of earthquakes and tornados), increase in violence, wide spread sickness and disease. However, two of the biggest changes, the maneuvering of political powers around the world to bring about a one world government and the attack on American culture are going unnoticed.

The second is so important because America is the last stronghold of a culture that is closest to the Kingdom Culture of the 1st and 2nd Century as displayed by the followers of Jesus Christ. Satan has succeeded in destroying faith in Christ throughout most of the world. There are pockets of Christ's followers but the most influential is found in the culture of the USA.

The culture of America is based on the Constitution that recognizes that their Creator endows its citizens with certain unalienable rights. Its laws are based on Biblical tradition. Two other aspects of its strength has been (1) the family unit that has been the cornerstone of the fabric of its society and (2) the majority of its citizens have had, until recently, knowledge of the Bible. Because of this God has prospered His people.

Jesus said, *"I will build my Church and the gates of hell will not prevail against it."* Therefore, it is up to His Church to extend His Kingdom throughout the world, making known this mystery by the power of the Holy Spirit. It is the responsibility of the Church to preach the Gospel of the Kingdom of God; not to preach only, however, but to live it out in their daily lives. This living out is expressed in the culture of the Kingdom.

Satan has successfully destroyed any resemblance to Kingdom Culture throughout the kingdoms of this world. Now, he is using every deceitful tactic and strategy to dismantle the culture of the USA. This battle is of significant importance to the Church and its mandate to extend the Kingdom of God because of the reasons stated above.

The battle is for the minds of men because it is in the mind that decisions are made has to how a person will live their life. It is in the mind that people make judgments about what they will accept in to their spirit. That in turn affects who will be their master and whom they will worship.

This first book will set the stage for you to understand what is necessary for you to be an Overcomer as Satan tries to destroy your faith while the crisis and the chaos approaches closer each day. This book will show you the seven elements of Kingdom Culture and give you a vision of what God has planned for His people.

Introduction

You might have picked up this first book of a two-volume set, thinking that the Abundant Life is a life of *receiving* when in fact it is just the opposite; it is a life of *giving*. It is a life full of battles but it is ultimately an overcoming life. It is to the Overcomer that Jesus our Savior King presents the greatest rewards. The one who says He is the first and the last, who was dead and is now alive for evermore makes these promises to the Overcomer:

- You shall eat of the Tree of Life that is in the midst of the paradise of God
- You shall not be hurt by the second death
- You shall receive some of the hidden manna, a white stone whereon is written a new name
- You shall receive power over the nations
- You will be clothed in white garments and your name, He will not blot out from the Book of Life
- You will be made a pillar in the temple of His God (the Father)
- You will be granted to sit with Him on His throne as He overcame and sat down with His Father

Why write this two-volume work on becoming and being an Overcomer at this time is history? It is because there has never been a time when the forces of evil are coming together to destroy the peoples of the God as they are today. The wicked are using all the deceitful tactics of the evil One to drown out the voice of righteousness throughout the world. The Church of the Lord Jesus Christ has been infiltrated by compromise and humanism and is no longer the voice of God heralding the words of Christ, *"Repent for the Kingdom of God is at hand."*

Dull of Hearing

What has happened to the Church universal, but especially in the USA, is the same as what we see recorded in the Book of Hebrews regarding the Jewish Christians. They had become

1

"dull of hearing". The writer of Hebrews wanted to explain more fully the mysteries of the Kingdom but his readers had become sluggish in their reception. They had become lazy in their faith; therefore, they were considered babes needing milk, unable to digest the meat of the Word. They needed someone to teach them again the first principles. The writer chastises them saying they are unskillful, unable to take in solid food. He says solid food is for those who are of full age.

The writer of Hebrews is pointing out to his readers the need for Spiritual Discernment. In other words, they need to hear the voice of the Holy Spirit and to humble themselves to be led of the Spirit. These are the Believers who are recognized as mature and who have become Overcomers.

It is not those that hear only, that are mature, but those that do the Word of God. "Full age" refers to those that are mature due to habitual practice. Those of "full age" have made it a practice of obeying the message of righteousness and are able to discern good and evil. He encourages them to go on to perfection, meaning maturity.

The Apostle Paul prays for the Church at Ephesus, *"That the God of our Lord Jesus Christ, the Father of glory, may give to you the spirit of wisdom and revelation in the knowledge of Him, the eyes of your understanding being enlightened; that you may know..."* Paul was praying that the Church would not be "dull of hearing" but receive the Holy Spirit who is the spirit of wisdom and revelation and knowledge.

Paul is encouraging them to draw from the Holy Spirit in order that they might know what the hope of His calling is to them. Paul, like the writer of the book of Hebrews, knew his readers would be coming from different cultures.

These new Christians were filled with a thousand questions. Some, like the Jews, had a faith in God but now needed to believe in Jesus Christ as their Messiah. Others had questions because they were completely ignorant of God; how to worship Him, how to live righteously and many other details regarding the Kingdom of God.

These first century Disciples of Christ were now facing persecution and trials that could never have been anticipated. If they were to be Overcomers, what they believed had to be more than a preference; it had to become a conviction. They were facing the loss of friends and family, they were facing threats of imprisonment and even death. They needed a conviction within them that said, "What I believe is the absolute truth". Without that conviction, many would fall away and many did.

The Church today will soon be facing the same trails and persecution as the saints that have gone before us. But do not despair, you will find within the pages of this book, the principles that Jesus utilized in leading his followers through the process of Transformation, giving them the conviction to remain faithful to Jesus Christ. These same Kingdom Principles, when embraced, will cause you to remain faithful when hard trials come your way and when you are facing persecution.

Nevertheless, all of what is happening in the world today, the overthrowing of the world economies and the shaping of a one- world government, must occur as Satan is working his plan. The Scriptures themselves tell us in Rev 13:7-8 that, *"It was granted to him to make war with the saints and to overcome them. Moreover, authority was given him over every tribe, tongue, and nation. All who dwell on the earth will worship him, whose names have not been written in the Book of Life of the Lamb slain from the foundation of the world".*

Satan has perverted the Church culture so that it now resembles the culture of the individual church, whether it is Catholic, Baptist, Methodist or Assemblies of God. The culture that is within the Church is a now a mirror of the culture of the world.

Transformation

In the midst of all the chaos, God is raising up men, women and children to be Overcomers. If we look a little closer, however, we must conclude that all of the marvelous things that Overcomers accomplish are an overflowing of the person themselves. It is the inner person that we must examine, his

Introduction

character, his spirit, his involvement with his God. WHAT HE DOES IS -A RESULT OF WHO HE IS.

The making of an Overcomer is a little like a caterpillar turning into a butterfly. A caterpillar crawls upon the ground, over leaves and rocks. It can only see what is directly in front of it and only what is within fractions of an inch from its eyes.

What a contrast with the butterfly that has the freedom of the air. It can fly over the tops of trees and from flower to flower. Children and adults alike admire it for its beauty. It knows nothing of the confinement that is the life of the caterpillar.

When the caterpillar shuts itself away in its cocoon, it has no idea what will become of it or what it will be transformed into. We are not sure what exactly happens inside that cocoon, but this we do know; the caterpillar undergoes a transformation that will affect its life forever, never to become a caterpillar again.

We will also undergo a transformation when we become an Overcomer for Jesus Christ. However, unlike the caterpillar and the butterfly, which go through this change as a part of nature, we have made a deliberate decision. We willingly lay down our "self" life in order to live the life of another. This transformation, like that of the caterpillar, will also affect our lives forever; we will never be the same person again.

This Transformation process is also like that of transforming an original 1932 Ford coupe into a V8 powered chopped and channeled Hot Rod. Once it is complete, you cannot undo and start over. This transformation is so much different from just adding a fancy paint job, mag wheels and leather interior. Those are just changes. God is not interested in changing us. He is interested in transforming us into His image.

The Transformation begins with our *involvement*. This is when we embrace the heart of the Father and align ourselves with His Grand Plan. Just as the caterpillar could no longer exist in order for the butterfly to come forth, so "self" can no longer exist in order for the "new Man in Christ Jesus" to come forth.

As we come to know Christ intimately "in us", His character will be revealed through our actions and our words. Others will look at us as if they are seeing Jesus. Jesus was a man of great faith; signs and wonders followed Him. As we strive to "know Him", our faith will also grow and the "works of God" will follow us!

What is it that determines our willingness to let the Holy Spirit transform us? Maybe Jesus had the answer when He said this about the woman caught in adultery, *"Wherefore I say unto you, her sins, which are many, are forgiven; for she loved much: but to whom little is forgiven, the same loves little"*.

Paul reveals this truth about the beginnings of the transformation process in 2 Cor 7:9, 11, *"Now I rejoice, not that you were made sorry, but that your sorrow led to repentance. For you were made sorry in a godly manner... For godly sorrow produces repentance leading to salvation, not to be regretted; but the sorrow of the world produces death.*

What diligence it produced in you, what clearing of yourselves, what indignation, what fear, what vehement desire, what zeal, what vindication!"

This first volume is written to help you learn to be lead by the Holy Spirit. God tells us that when we become a son of God it is because we are lead by the Spirit. In order words, to be lead of the Spirit is to mature. This is a process but it begins by having a kingdom mindset. By the grace of God, this is what I hope it impart to you. By involving yourself in this transformation process you will partake in the joy of participating in Kingdom Living.

This book will encourage, motivate, and equip you to walk in greater maturity, wisdom, character, holiness and power. Inspired by Jesus' mentoring of His disciples, you will be equipped and prepared to become a passionate builder of God's Kingdom.

Introduction

Six things to keep in mind as you read this book:

- Our walk with God is all about Relationship that leads into Fellowship.

- All truths are parallel (spiritual truths are found in the physical realm revealing the truths of the spiritual). Because of this, we can clearly and easily understand our God.

- The *all* importance of having a Kingdom Mindset

- It is the Holy Spirit that Transforms (Maturity) and Empowers (Overcoming).

- A SHOEBOX APPROACH - I HAVE BEEN TEACHING THIS COURSE FOR MANY YEARS. THERE ARE SOME SECTIONS THAT MY STUDENTS HAVE FOUND MORE DIFFICULT TO UNDERSTAND OR ACCEPT. THESE SECTIONS ARE FORMATTED WITH SMALL CAPS. DO NOT AUTOMATICALLY DISCARD THE INFORMATION IF YOU FIND IT DIFFICULT TO PROCESS. I ENCOURAGE YOU TO SET ASIDE THIS INFORMATION. IT MAY HELP TO PUT IT IN A SHOEBOX ON A SHELF TO BE CONSIDERED LATER. This is OK; I've been doing it for years.

- Some things are very important for your understanding. When you see this shaded background, stop and reread the material to make sure you fully comprehend its meaning. If not then put it in your shoebox.

If you are a new "born again" Believer, you might find it helpful to begin with Kingdom Worldview, page 147

Chapter One

What in the World are You Looking At?

Shaping a Worldview

Every event you experience in life shapes your *worldview* or *understanding of life.* It develops and takes shape and forms over time. As you grow spiritually, physically, mentally and socially, so does the formation of your worldview. We all perceive our world differently because of our differences of where we live, our education experiences, upbringing, and from what we hear from people we respect. Some of us cannot define or defend our worldview because we have never thought about it, we have just absorbed it from the influences that surround us.

The needs and wants (that often come from the above experiences) are what we deem most important and drive the development of our own personal worldview. We use up large amounts of time, energy, and money traveling down many pathways that lead to nowhere because we really don't know what is of prime importance to us. Our motivation has always been confused between our wants and our needs.

There are survival needs that keep body and soul together; these we all have. Then there are wants, which for some people go so deep it causes them to be driven, such as money, knowledge, fame, recognition, freedom, influence, power and health. Jesus gave us what we should be seeking when He said, *"Seek first the kingdom of God and HIS righteousness."*

Our worldview, whether religious or not, is a personal insight about reality and the meaning of life. It is often termed a "Life Understanding". It develops in part because we have sought some understanding of our own significance.

Whatever we do, we must come to that place where we agree within ourselves that what we believe to be the truth, is correct or at least without consequences. If we do not, we are in disagreement with ourselves and when that happens, we can have no inner peace.

A worldview is a set of presuppositions (or assumptions) which we hold (consciously or subconsciously) about the basic makeup of our world.[1] A worldview is, first of all, an explanation and interpretation of the world and second, an application of this view to life.[2] A worldview provides a model of the world which guides its adherents in the world.[3] Whichever one you prefer, of the three before mentioned definitions, it comes down to this: Our worldview is ever changing until we come to that place in life when we are at peace with ourselves in what we believe.

All worldviews or understandings of life are based on assumptions. Assumptions are beliefs without proof or something taken for granted. It is from these assumptions that we believe something is true or false, or somewhere in- between.

The problem is; those assumptions, upon which we base our understanding of life, often go unchallenged. Therefore, we base our thoughts, feelings, and actions on false assumptions. Assumptions that are based on incomplete or faulty knowledge can and will most likely result in wrong conclusions.

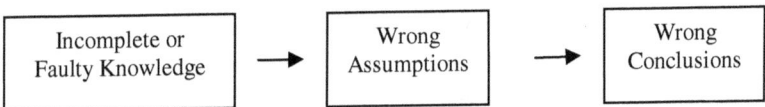

Incomplete or Faulty Knowledge	→	Wrong Assumptions	→	Wrong Conclusions

Culture: Prime source for our Worldview

The prime source for the development of our worldview comes from the culture of which we are a part. Cultures are described as the learned and shared patterns of information that a group uses to generate meaning among its members.

Within larger cultures such as that of a nation, city and region, there are also smaller cultures. In these smaller cultures, the members share beliefs in certain rules, gender roles, behaviors, religious beliefs and values. These cultural values combine to shape the individual's worldview and influence their interaction with others.

This is the point to comprehend, OVERCOMERS ARE THE PRODUCT OF THEIR CULTURE. You don't find apples on an orange tree. Neither do you find Overcomers coming from a church that is more concerned with helping people to get a hold of the best life now or becoming a force for social change.

Culture is a breeding ground for the character of the people in that particular culture; therefore, choosing the correct culture in which to cultivate our worldview is of prime importance. Our culture is a major factor in determining what is important to us and then driving us to achieve.

Unknowingly we are forming our worldview, whether we recognize it or not, because we need a worldview to:

- Unify our thoughts about life
- Define the good life, that we might find hope and meaning in life
- Guide our dreams regarding our future
- Guide our actions

The Battle for the Mind

There is a conflict going on for our worldview. So what part does the MIND play in winning or losing the battle? The mind is the control center for all our dreams, hopes, fears and faith. It is here that we make decisions and vocalize what is in our heart. The mind is the center of our consciousness that generates thoughts, feelings, ideas, and stores knowledge and memories.

The Bible speaks of the Sound Mind, the Carnal Mind, the Blinded Mind, the Darkened Mind, and the Reprobate Mind. The Bible gives over 60 references to the word "think". Thinking is a process of the mind whereby we consider ideas and make judgments.

The mind is the collection point for the five senses as well as the spiritual influences, which enlists our will, emotions and body to perform acts that the mind has approved. Before we were converted and were "born again", the spirit of this world had full access to our mind. However, if we were brought up in the church, the Word of God could have affected our conscience and influenced our thoughts and behavior.

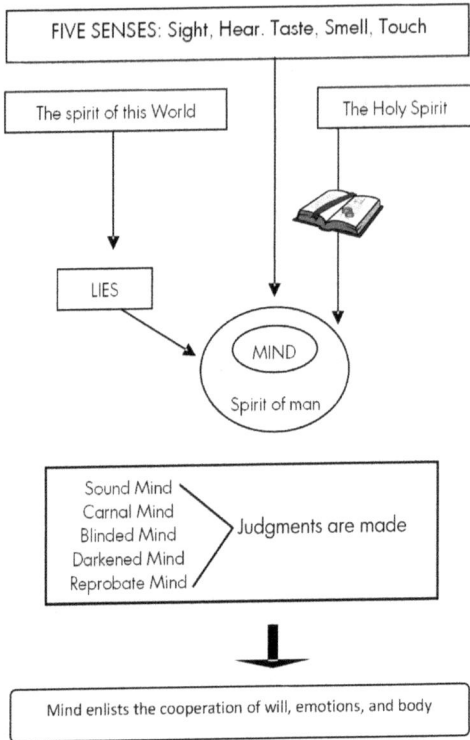

Satan's ultimate goal is to deceive us so that we willingly break the contract, the covenant that we have with God. This breaking of the covenant on our part results in the same loss of fellowship that Adam and Eve experienced in the Garden of Eden. Importantly, it is here that Satan wants to move us away from living a Kingdom culture to living a worldly culture.

The conflict is not between Jesus and Satan; that battle is already won. The real conflict rages here on earth between different worldviews that contend for our affection.

Satan knows that unless a Christian chooses and embraces a Kingdom Worldview and travels through the straight and narrow way, he is open prey that can be snared. Read what the

Holy Spirit says about the Seven Churches in the Book of Revelation as they deviated from the Plan that God had for them:

Ephesus	- The loveless Church
Smyma	- The Persecuted Church
Pergamos	- The Compromising Church
Thyatira	- The Corrupt Church
Sardis	- The Dead Church
Laodicea	- The Luke warm Church
Philadelphia	- The Faithful Church

As information is brought into the mind by our five senses and through our spirit, it finds a place to attach itself. If not, it is dismissed. We then make basic assumptions about the meaning of life, death, relationships and a million other things that ultimately affect our behavior. This behavior is reinforced day after day until challenged.

Why is it so hard for Christians and non-Christians to accept new ideas? Let us use a jar of jellybeans to try to understand our problem. Each of the jellybeans can represent a position (acceptance of a presupposition) that we have taken, that covers a million issues in life. They can range from our favorite color to being a Muslim or a Christian. It can be from the kind of car we would like to drive to the type of person we want to marry. It could be a spiritual position, a philosophical position, it could be a social or an economic position we have taken.

These positions are accepted as truth. If not, then a conflict would arise within us and self-preservation does not allow this. The more firmly we accept our position as truth the more we are willing to defend it and even fight for it.

If the jellybeans (our positions on issues) are loosely packed inside the jar, another jellybean can easily take its place when challenged. Therefore, if we hold lightly to some truths, our positions or beliefs regarding those truths can constantly be changing throughout our lives.

If on the other hand, the jellybeans are packed tightly together, it then becomes much harder to displace one with another. This solidification of our presuppositions is sure to happen when we experience deep emotional, physical, social, and financial or even spiritual traumas. These traumas can come through nature (war, fire, hurricanes, and earthquakes), our personal environment (rape, robbery and assault), our education, or our family (divorce, separation or murder).

Again, if the truths we believe in strongly are a result of some traumatic experience, or come from someone we highly respect and trust or come from our prized education; these positions then have come about as from heat and are held together as if by super glue. This is like the jar of jellybeans that is left out in the sun and the heat has more or less cemented the jellybeans together.

Can you define your worldview? Are your jellybeans glued together so that no new thought has an opportunity to affect your life? Are you operating on incomplete or faulty knowledge?

---

[1] James Sire
[2] Phillips and Brown
[3] Walsh and Middleton

Chapter Two

How Do You See It?

Changing Our Worldview

Our motive and goal in this book is that we all may "see" God the Father, how all things are related to Him and to His purpose. In order to receive benefit from this study however, it may require a change in our worldview. How then does a change in our worldview come about? Adults are most open to new ideas when those new ideas speak about things that are most important to them. We must understand; no change in our worldview can occur unless there is acknowledgement that our current view is wrong or at least based on insufficient information.

Jesus appeared to Paul on the road to Damascus; Peter heard the rooster crow three times; Peter had a vision on a roof top; King David had a finger pointed at him; Moses had two Hebrew men question his motive. In each of these cases, there had to be a rectification in their philosophy or Worldview. There was a pivotal moment that caused them to reflect upon and assess their presuppositions.

For too long we have been spoon-fed doctrine and told to, "just believe". We have been searching for a more meaningful life by attending conferences, changing churches, etc. without knowing that our searching must be for a deeper relationship with the Holy Spirit, who is the revealer of all truth.

The present world crisis is bringing people into the Church, some for the first time and many are coming in from other religious backgrounds. As they come in, they bring in enormous amounts of wrong thinking that must be changed if they are going to put the puzzle of life together and have abundant life. There must be a modification in their worldview in order for them to be successful in their Christian walk.

A Challenged Worldview

Dr. C. E. Fast, gave his life to Jesus Christ before he was 10 years old. He went on to college and then to Seminary where he earned his three Doctorate degrees and later in life he was awarded two honorary Doctorate degrees. He grew in prominence in his denomination and served the Lord in the largest Baptist church in Zion, IL. His reputation allowed him to serve in other high positions within his denomination as well.

The problem reared its ugly head when his wife, Edna, was introduced to a magazine published by The Full Gospel Businessman's Fellowship International. The small magazine presented articles about the Baptism in the Holy Spirit, speaking in other tongues and physical healings. Even though this was against what she had learned, something within the articles caused her to want to know more. She needed to learn more in order to satisfy the hunger that was now consuming her. She soon found herself speaking in other tongues and sharing her new experience with other women in her Baptist church.

Dr. Fast found himself in hot water when the church board found out what Mrs. Fast was doing. They quickly went to him and presented an ultimatum; have Mrs. Fast stop what she was doing (sharing her experience with other women) and renounce it as evil or they would force him to resign.

It is important to understand that Dr. Fast preached against this experience all his life. He did not have the experience himself nor did he desire it. He found himself in a very difficult situation. What was he to do? On the one hand, he could not deny the change he witnessed in his wife but on the other hand, everything within him said it was wrong. He would have to choose between the teachings he had received from his childhood through Seminary plus his own studies and his wife's newfound experience with the Holy Spirit.

If he chose to go along with the church board he would save his reputation, his standing within the denomination, and his pension (he was in his late fifties now). If he sided with his wife, he would lose his position in the church and all doors would be closed to him to pastor another church in the Baptist organization. To compound that issue, he himself did not have nor did he desire the experience therefore, the Charismatic and Pentecostals would have no need for him either.

He chose to go against the wishes of the church board. Even though he did not agree or accept for himself the experience as explained to him by his wife, he could not deny the new relationship she now had with the Holy Spirit. There was just too much academia, too much Baptist theology to overcome for him to accept it for himself.

Two long years went by of being a pastor without a church and being ostracized by former colleagues and friends. It was not until the Full Gospel Businessmen Fellowship International (FGBFI) had a retreat in Green Lakes, WI that Dr. Fast finally laid aside his Seminary training and opened his mind and heart. After three days of testimony and much prayer by others, he received that which he preciously renounced.

He was finally able to exchange some jellybeans for others; jellybeans that had been cemented together by academics and years of preaching. For the rest of his life, God began to use Dr. Fast in supernatural and miraculous ways. His life affected hundreds of young men and women, including myself. Yes, these new jellybeans changed his life up until the day he died.

An Experimental Worldview

At the age of seventeen, Joni Eareckson Tada, became paralyzed because of an accident. She prayed for healing. However, she has remained confined to a wheelchair as a quadriplegic. When you read Joni's story you can do nothing but admire her. She has found meaning and purpose in her life despite all of the suffering, heartache and disappointments. We read in her story how God can work for our good and give us peace in the place which we come to accept.

She has developed a sensitive heart toward others who find themselves in similar conditions and has given them courage to go on and become productive, in spite of their circumstances. I can understand the position that she has come to regarding her paralysis. The following account is from an article that appeared in Moody Magazine, "Among Friends—Healing". It is a story of her struggle with faith.[1]

"The following event occurred after relating the story of her friend who was supernaturally healed. She asked, "Does this mean arise and walk miracles are for everyone?" Then she asks her audience, "Is God obliged to cure every sick person? I don't think so. The Bible doesn't teach it, and experience doesn't support it."

In terms of prayer, Joni states, "God gives two conditions if our prayers are to be guaranteed answers. We must be living in close fellowship with Him, and our requests must be in line with His will. Because God hasn't chosen to reveal every detail of His will to Christians, then we must leave our requests in His hands."

Joni says further, "It's more likely that he will glorify Himself through our suffering and this is quite a miracle. What if you are a Christian who is really trying to abide in Christ and you're still beyond a cure? If this is you, you're not alone. I can identify. But after looking everywhere else for reasons why my prayers were not answered, I returned to God's Word for a closer look. It was there I found something that shed light on not only the healing question, but also on the whole issue of why Christians suffer. If you have tried everything to be healed but nothing has changed, then has it ever really hit you that the reason you are in your present condition is that God, in His wisdom, wills it to be so?"

Joni has concluded, "Because God hasn't chosen to reveal every detail of his will to Christians, then we must leave our requests in his hands. He may remove suffering as a kind of sneak preview of coming attractions but it's more likely that He will glorify Himself through our suffering. And that is quite a miracle."

In the years following Joni's accident, her beliefs regarding healing and God's will solidified. They became as a jellybean jar sitting in the sun; the jellybeans melted together and nothing now or ever is going to change her position dealing with healing or in regards to human suffering in general. Joni had come to the place where she believed that she ("is beyond a cure") and that her condition is God's will. She can live with that (be at peace with herself). Here is the point to remember: We can go no farther than our Faith will take us. Joni has reached the limit of her Faith. We will and can act only on what we believe.

When we are predisposed to find our answers only within the realm of what is already accepted and unwilling to step outside our present worldview, we will accept anything whether it is true or not.

You will find our response to Joni's assertions on page 160

A Circumstantial Worldview

Stan is a Jewish man who grew up in New York City. In his home, he heard the stories that relived the horrors of the holocaust from his relatives. He is an Ivy League University MBA graduate whose family has come to believe God has abandoned the Jewish people. The stories of aunts and uncles that had witnessed the horror of Nazi Germany made a big impression on all of his family. He vividly remembers stories of how the Rabbis' fasted for weeks and prayed 24 hours a day, for days, only to become disillusioned when "their God had shut his ears to their cry".

At the telling of each story, another brick was added to the wall that was beginning to surround Stan's heart. It was not long before the wall was finished and he had sealed off any love for God that could penetrate his mind and heart. Stan still thinks of himself as a Jew. He observes all the Jewish holidays and even fasts on holy days. There is, however, no love for a God that did nothing for the Jewish people during those horrible days of the holocaust.

The stories from people Stan loves and trusts, plus the plain picture of history confirmed what he already had accepted as true. His jellybeans melted together and nothing is going to break them apart. The wall is built and no one can tear it down. He has closed his ears to everything except what he already has agreed to within himself.

Seeking your Worldview

The three foregoing stories model the case in point that it is difficult for us to change our worldview. We have already said

17

that in order for us to find what our heart truly desires outside our present worldview, we must humble ourselves and be open to something new. It also demands a relationship with the Holy Spirit where by we are submissive to His leading.

Man is by nature curious. Nevertheless, because there is so much information out there, we cannot possibly digest it all. Because there is all this information and no central command post to filter out the truth from the false, many well intentioned Christians are being exposed to thoughts and ideas that sound true and good but are producing within them a watered down man-centered Biblical worldview. This incomplete worldview will lead to wrong conclusions and will keep them from maturing. While we must remain cautious, we must also be curious.

We have said earlier that what we consider most important in our lives will drive our search for a worldview. What we really desire, even if we don't realize it, is dominion. Nevertheless, dominion is something that, either you have it or you do not. You are in control or you are not. We have to ask then; do men and women really know what is important for them to have?

We might have a limited form of control or dominion over our lives but it is only limited. Since man lost his dominion over the earth, he has been struggling and searching for the next best thing: freedom. However, to have freedom we must understand that freedom is a gift and is only given by the One who has ultimate control: the one in POWER.

How we think, act, and feel, comes from how we understand life—our worldview. It is the differences in our worldviews that lead us down different paths to what we believe is the place or the state of mind where we can find this freedom. It is our journey to find freedom that will absorb all our energy and tax our ability and our heart. We all want to be free but Man without a Kingdom worldview will always come to the wrong conclusion.

We seek to be free from our daily grind, a job that we hate the pain in our body, the pressures and stress of the job or family, the feelings of hopelessness, purposelessness, depression, and defeat, the worry of finances, children and sickness, the over-whelming guilt of adultery, pornography, lesbianism or homosexuality and any other sin in our life. Men and women want to be free from the bad relationships that they are locked into and from the control of others.

We want to be free to do what we want. We want to be able to choose the sacrifices that we will make. We want to be free to choose how we will spend our time and money and whom we will love or not love. We all want to be free but man, without God, will always come to the wrong conclusions.

Change a culture, change a Worldview

The pathway that we take to find our freedom is more often, predetermined by our culture. When we come into the Church, we try to blend two cultures together, the World and the Kingdom. However, this does not work. There can be no compromise. One culture will always try to dominate the other.

The United States has been called the "Melting Pot" of the world. This designation came about because when people from all over the world came to the USA they did not establish cultural ghettos, they adapted to the language, norms and values that were already in place.

The reason so many people wanted and still want to come to the USA is base on the foundational principles that this country was built upon. The constitution said that each individual had rights given to them by their Creator that could not be taken away. The money is stamped with, "In God we trust". The pledge to the flag states that we are "one nation under God". The major universities were started to provide education to those studying for church ministry. Hospitals were started by churches to care for the sick. Schools used the Bible to promote reading and ethics. Even as late as 1958 schools gave early release to students, myself included, to attend religious education classes where they learned the major doctrines, creeds and tents of their faith.

Where is the clarity of American culture today? The above traditions are all but gone and so is our connection to the past. The United States was not so much a Christian nation but a nation that feared God. The Bible says the beginning of wisdom is the fear of God. It was not by accident therefore, that the USA became the greatest nation in recent times.

There are those in the world that want to keep the waters muddy and the eyes of our understanding blind when it comes to culture. There are those in our world that have fostered the idea of Multiculturalism, the belief that all cultures and beliefs are of equal value and equal validity.

The truth is that cultures, other than Kingdom culture, fail to provide a vision of society to which there is faith, hope and love. They fail to offer a way of life for people from every race or economic and educational status to come and enjoy true abundant life. Kingdom culture is the only culture that so appeals to the heart of man that he will give all to obtain a right to be a part of it.

Please do not misunderstand me; the culture of the USA is not Kingdom culture. It does, however, allow the Church of Jesus Christ to openly reveal Kingdom culture to the world, hence the attack against America. The true attack, therefore, is really against God Himself.

Satan's attack on the culture of the Kingdom of God is deliberate and focused. He has one thing in mind; that is for him to retain and to even expand his kingdom and to finally include all earthly kingdoms under one rule; his. His kingdom is a kingdom of lawlessness while God's Kingdom is one of righteousness. Therefore, he is out to eliminate righteous living in the world.

Because of this, knowing Kingdom Culture is of the upmost importance. We must know how to respond when we find ourselves in situations like the above and to help others to find hope and freedom.

---

[1] Joni Eareckson Tada, "Among Friends—Healing" Moody Magazine

Chapter Three

Culturally Correct

Making the Kingdom Connection

Have you ever worked on a 5,000-piece puzzle only to find it is next to impossible to put it together without a picture or at least have some clue to what it looks like? Even the picture must resemble something that we are familiar with or at least something, we can recognize. It is very much the same with life. We need a framework that ties everything together, something that allows us to understand our society, the world, and our place in it. It must help us to make the critical decisions, which will shape our own individual future. That framework is CULTURE.

George Barna in his 1993 book, *Turn-Around Churches*,[1] describes why he thinks some churches are growing and some are declining. In discussing the resistance to change he states, "Stalwarts in a dying church often argue that things will return to normal if the church can do a better job of doing what it has always done." On the other side of the coin, however, what he also found was that, "pastors of the new mega-churches attribute a significant part of their impact and growth to studying the ministry terrain and adapting their ministry practices to the needs and realities of the community context without undermining their theological beliefs."

The problem is that both views do not take into consideration the culture of the Kingdom that must be lived out. Both are trying to use religion as a means to meet the needs of people. They are both using a failed belief system as the foundation of their own brand of culture they are sprouting. By doing so, they are only adding to the division amongst God's people and still are not answering the deepest questions and longings of the human soul.

Christianity, as a religion and as it is experienced today in the Western world, is not the answer. Millions have left 'The

Faith' to become agnostics, atheists, or adherents to non-Christian religions or cults. The Church has failed to make the Kingdom Connection. Christianity may be a religion but the Church is a community of the "called out" that are living for their King in a culture that He ordered and designed for His people.

Culture is a shared, learned, symbolic system of values, beliefs and attitudes. It is that which shapes and influences our perception and behavior—an abstract "mental blueprint" or "mental code." It is what shapes our worldview.

- Culture is something learned; it does not happen overnight. It is a process.
- The members of a society share culture. There is No "culture of one." This is important as it relates to the Church and our being involved in the Church.
- Culture has a pattern. People in a society live and think in ways that form definite patterns and are distinguished from other societies.
- Cultures are mutually constructed by all members of a society through a constant process of social interaction.
- Cultures come about through language and thought therefore they are figurative in nature.
- Cultures are arbitrary. They are not based on "natural laws" but are created, usually at the direction of those who are leading the society.
- Cultures are internalized; Worldviews (behaviors, attitudes, values) become Habitual. They are taken-for-granted and perceived as "natural."[2]

In order to win the conflict for a worldview that enables us to have an abundant life and to be an effective minister, we must understand the Culture of the Kingdom of God. To do this we must know how it all connects to having a kingdom mind-set.

God has given to humanity, two institutions to make sure we have the structure that will enable us to have an understanding of the seven basic elements (covered in Chapter four) that make up the culture of the Kingdom of God. These two institutions that affect our culture and therefore our worldview are church and family.

The world is trying to use religion as a belief system to answer the questions regarding life, the purpose of life and the unknown of death. Like a puzzle, mankind's world has fallen apart and he has been trying to fit all the pieces back together again with the same results as Humpy Dumpy. The Church without Kingdom Culture is no different that of any other religion.

Humpty Dumpty

Humpty Dumpty sat on a wall,
Humpty Dumpty had a great fall.
All the King's horses, And all the King's men
Couldn't put Humpty together again!

Catching the Wind

The responsibility of fashioning Kingdom Culture has been given to the Holy Spirit. Just as He was given the responsibility of bringing the creative Word from heaven to form the heavens and the earth, so He is shaping and molding the culture of the Kingdom into the life of the Church.

He does not work alone, however, so in order for the Church to complete its assignment, Jesus gave Apostles, Prophets, Evangelist, Pastor and Teachers. This five-fold ministry team is charged with the task of making sure the culture of the Kingdom of God is extended throughout the whole earth. The reason, for the five-fold ministry, is so that the responsibility does not rest on anyone person. Each member of the team has a part to perform in the bringing the body of Christ to maturity.

The mandate that goes to the five-fold ministry is to EQUIP the saints. They are to prepare the saints to hear the voice, or sense in their spirit, the leading of the Holy Spirit and act according. The Holy Spirit is the power of God to create, fashion, transform and empower. If the five-fold ministry is limited in any way, we limit the work of the Holy Spirit. Without the work of the Holy Spirit, the preacher's words fall on ears that cannot hear.

The best way I know how to relate this is by a personal experience. When I was ministering in the Finger Lakes region of New York State, my son, Steve and I bought a small sailboat. One day, he and I went out to Seneca Lake at Geneva, N.Y. Seneca Lake is a spring fed; cold and deep lake nestled between two hills. Because of this, strong gusts of wind would suddenly sweep down over the water and catch many unsuspecting, untrained, unqualified and unwary sailors unprepared for the danger that could lie ahead. Of course, I'm speaking of myself.

The sail is the heart of a sailboat. Without the sail, a boat is dead in the water. But, what is more important to a sailor is the wind. The wind causes the boat to move and fulfill its purpose. It is the skill of the sailor, however, that determines the direction and speed of the boat, because he determines the sail's ability to catch the wind. Even when there is only a little wind or even when there is not a favorable wind, a good sailor can go forward by adjusting the sail.

The purpose of the five-fold ministry, in its simplest terms, is this: They are to help the members of the body of Christ to 'Catch the Wind'. In this simple act, they are demonstrating to the Church their own submission to the Holy Spirit and are being an example to the saints.

We must not ignore the gifts that Christ has given to the Church. The local church must not now proudly promote the fact that they (the local church) are sovereign in their government. In other words, they do not need oversight and they can direct the teaching of God's Word as they see fit. They must not see themselves as having a pastor, a board and that is all they need.

When the above happens, church leadership establishes its own culture; whether it is denominational, independent, or inter-denominational or just a local gathering meeting in the name of Jesus. Even Churches that recognized apostolic authority can fall prey to setting up their own culture if the Apostle does all the preaching and does not set up pastors in order to build up the body of Christ. Why is this so, because his calling (grace) is different from that of a pastor?

The majority of Churches have opted to teach everything under the sun EXCEPT kingdom culture. Is it any wonder that we are where we are with no power and no vision for the future except heaven? If we are truthful with ourselves, we must admit that we can hardly recognize any difference when the Church is compared with the world.

For more insight into the five-fold ministry see my second book, *A KINGDOM WHICH CANNOT BE SHAKEN.*

---

[1] George Barna, *Turn-Around Churches,* Introduction page 12

[2] The definition of culture came from a variety of sources with no one source making a major contribution

Chapter Four

Seven Elements of Culture

Kingdom Culture

A kingdom has no stronger influence upon another than through its culture. Its values, morals, citizen behavior, dress codes, music, religious practices and more express who they are and even more so, who they represent. Jesus made known the power, the quality of life, and the blessings of being connected to His kingdom. His Kingdom Culture offers to all the citizens a way to experience it. We are to do the same.

Seven basic elements make up a culture, any culture and these are what we want to focus on. They are: Government, Economic System, Social Organization, Customs and Tradition, Language, Art and Literature, and Religion.

Even though Government and Economic System are not included in the definition given by Sociologists, these two elements influence and therefore determine the shape of culture more than anything else. I came to this conclusion while traveling overseas and paying particular attention to the culture of the country in which I was ministering.

What I also concluded was that; it is the primary responsibility of the Church of the Lord Jesus Christ to explain and demonstrate the culture of the Kingdom of God. Everything else church leaders do is of lesser significance. The Church has preached on these topics from time to time but they have failed to make the Kingdom connection.

1. Government

The king makes his will and desires known through a government that he creates. Whoever rules over a government, exercising its authority, is the one that has the most powerful influence on the kingdom's culture. The government does so by controlling and administering public policy that will affect all members of the society.

The foundation that the kingdom of God is built upon is righteousness. Righteousness is the golden thread that is woven into every fabric of the kingdom. It is the factor that influences all the motives, thoughts, feelings, and actions of the king and the citizens of the kingdom.

In the Kingdom of God, our governmental ruler is Jesus Christ. He is our King. He sits on the throne of His Father and rules, not the earth, but the affairs of its citizens. He rules the hearts of those that have entered into the Kingdom by being "born again." The dominion of the earth has been given to the citizens of the Kingdom who then use His authority to govern or have dominion over the earth. All authority is His and His alone; we are to use it to carry out His Father's will here on earth.

To function within the Kingdom of God, we must understand how God's government operates. The following Chapter will give a description of the nine fundamental activities of government.

2. Economic System

FAITH is at the heart of our relationship with God our Father, Our King Jesus Christ and the Spirit of God. It is also, what makes the Kingdom of God run. Unfortunately, faith has been studied and used as if it is a separate entity or doctrine. FAITH is like the engine that keeps the train moving. Without FAITH, nothing happens in the Kingdom of God. God operates by FAITH. Even in Creation, the Word was spoken and by faith, the worlds were created. We need to see FAITH as it operates in every aspect of kingdom life.

The Word of God cannot affect the lives of the citizens of the Kingdom without the principles (teachings and guidelines) that it presents being lived out in FAITH. The Just shall live by FAITH is the theme of the Bible. It is by Faith that the righteous are led by the Spirit of God and it is those that are led by the Spirit of God that are the sons of God.

FAITH is also the medium of exchange (something commonly recognized as having a standard of value and used in the same way as money, e.g. gold) in the Kingdom. FAITH is not just about believing, but about exchange. FAITH is a spiritual commodity. It does not belong to the earth. It is heavenly.

Every culture has a medium of exchange, whether it is gold, silver, potatoes or paper money. It is what that culture recognizes as having great value and can be used as a means of exchange throughout that nation, country or kingdom. No nation can exist without a medium of exchange.

When I was in Poland, before the Iron Curtain came down, I could not buy anything with American dollars except at what they called "Dollar stores". It was illegal for the citizens to have "Dollars". I could only use their "Zylote" to purchase items that I wanted. In every country where I have gone it is the same; I could use only the currency that is acceptable and recognized.

The principle is the same in the Kingdom of God where the medium of exchange is FAITH. Faith is of the greatest value and even Peter said that is why our Faith is tested; to see its REAL value. Is it fool's gold, 8 carets, 10, 14, 18 or 21-carat gold?

Just as the quality of our FAITH is important, so is the quantity of our FAITH. How much faith do you have, no faith, a little faith, much faith? Jesus, the Son of God and our King said, *"According to your faith be it unto you!"* Jesus could do nothing but heal a FEW sick folk in Capernaum because there was no faith.

In this world, we are so used to using money as the medium of exchange that we don't know how to use Faith or how to operate it. We have reduced FAITH down to something we can understand; putting it in earthly or worldly terms. We understand it as a belief, a confidence, and a mental acceptance of something.

If you need a new roof for your house, you need the amount and quality of FAITH that will pay for the new roof. If you need a healing for cancer or a healing for a headache, you need what is required for each. Just because you were healed of a headache yesterday does not mean that the faith that you had yesterday will enable you receive a healing for a cancer today.

You get faith the same way you get money to pay a doctor bill; you work for it. There is only one source for FAITH; it comes from the same king that provides what you need, King Jesus. It is something like buying from the "company store". The company pays you for the work you have done and you buy what you need from the company.

The author and finisher of our FAITH is Jesus Christ. He is the Word made flesh. FAITH comes from the Word and as you spend more time mediating on the Word, allowing it to flood into your very soul (this is the *work* part), your heart begins to focus on the love and power of your King. Your hand now reaches out to receive what you've asked for because you know your faith is sufficient to cover the cost. Revelation springs up in your heart and you know that you know that God is pleased with your FAITH (quality and quantity).

There is another aspect involved in the economic system that goes along with FAITH. Jesus said, "Give and it shall be given back". Sacrificial giving is the heart of the Father; giving of oneself for another just as He demonstrated in the giving of His only begotten Son.

Much more is said on this important topic in my second book, *A Kingdom Which Cannot be Shaken*. See Chapter Four and the worksheet at the end of the book.

3. Social Organization

People that are a part of or submit to Kingdom Culture need to connect to others of like attitude and mind-set. We individually are saved by grace but together—we subject our wills to the will of our King; and say to our Father in heaven, "*not my will but yours be done*". It is together that we fulfill the purpose for which we are created.

Culture comprises many things but the bottom-line is that it is all about relationships. Therefore, when outsiders to the culture of the Kingdom are given the opportunity to look into the Kingdom, what they see is something that is a complete opposite to the culture of this world.

The first relationship we see in Scripture is that of the family. God created Adam and gave to him a wife. God told them, "*Be fruitful and multiply; fill the earth and subdue it; have dominion over the fish of the sea, over the birds of the air, and over every living thing that moves on the earth."* (Gen. 1:28).

God established the family unit to express Kingdom Culture. The family is to be FRUITFUL (fulfill its purpose), MULTIPLY (use its authority and creativity to produce, have plenty and bring in an abundance), FILL THE EARTH (increase the numbers of their family-fill the whole earth with their descendants), Subdue (bring it under subjection), and HAVE DOMINION (prevail against, reign, rule over).

Within this extended family culture, we see the love that Kingdom people have toward their king. We also see the love that the people have toward one another. They love even their enemies and do good toward them that hate them. What the outside world witnesses is Christ revealed in the saints of God as they are transformed into the image of their King.

4. Customs and Traditions

Customs usually come about because of events, location or personal likes or dislikes. Some customs are ordered by those in authority to give remembrance to great men or to God, while others just happen. The customs and traditions found in Kingdom Culture are a not a result of just a one-time event but are a result of habitual practice becoming the usual way of acting or responding in a given situation.

When our children see those in the Church living-out the culture of the Kingdom, they accept this behavior as NORMAL. When those in the world see this behavior, they recognize the cause and effect relationship—obedience brings blessing.

We hand down to the next generation our traditions regarding holidays and celebrations so that they have a connection to a lifestyle that we cherish. We hand down statements of belief and wisdom that will benefit and bring blessing to our children and pray that they will past these down to their children.

We cherish our Traditions because they link us to our past. Customs are important to us because they reveal and reinforce the principles and values by which we live. This is why the enemies of Christ wish to tear them down. I.e. School Prayer

5. Language

Language is more than just a means of communication. It greatly influences our culture by and through our thought processes because language predetermines what we see in the world around us. In other words, language acts like a polarizing lens on a camera in filtering reality—we see the real world only through the prism of our language because we can only understand our world through what we can express through our words.

YOU   +   YOUR LANGUAGE   =   YOUR REALITY

The Old Testament was written in Hebrew, which is a pictorial language. When a word is spoken, it almost immediately appears as a picture in your mind. While in the New Testament, which is written in Greek, a more precise meaning appears that differentiates it from another, it is more black and white.

The language of the Kingdom and the meaning of its words do not come from the earth but from heaven. Our communication comes from shared experiences, shared facts, ideas, and events that have been interpreted by the Holy Spirit. Worldly eyes have not seen nor did their ears hear what the spirit has revealed to us, the citizens of the Kingdom. Jesus spoke in parables so that those in the world would hear but not understand, would see but not comprehend.

Words, when translated into another language can have an entirely different meaning and convey something quite the opposite from that which was intended. I have found this to be very embarrassing when traveling in foreign countries when using an interpreter from a different country, but having the same language. Something, however, in the translation gives it another meaning; something that is offensive to the hearers in the country I'm in.

The Kingdom is for its citizens, not for the world. The Kingdom is for those that have entered into it by being "born again." The language of the Kingdom of God is what moves us and transforms us into the image of Christ. When we speak the Word, we enter the spiritual realm and with this in mind, we can have whatever we say. (See Mark 11:22-24).

6. Religion

Every culture has a religion that is accepted by the majority of people in a society. It gives people something to cling to when life brings events beyond their understanding. It consists of universal patterns of beliefs, values and behavior.

These patterns of a culture's religion are systematic because their manifestations are regular in occurrence and in expression and the majority of the members of that religion share them. Within all religions, however, not everyone complies with all the doctrines prescribed. There are differences of interpretation of the principles and meanings put forth. What is of great importance is that when the people have a close tie toward their leaders and with each other, their core beliefs are held more strongly.

All religions present to their adherents, symbols and rituals that make life meaningful. The Catholics kneel and make the sign of the cross when they come into the church sanctuary. Baptists dedicate babies.

Cultures endorse a system of religious symbols, along with religious actions to establish powerful, pervasive, and long lasting moods and motivations. In other words, these symbols help to construct how a society will view the world around them. It helps in providing a worldview that includes—a god.

7. Art and Literature

Art and literature are ways and means that we humans use to express what is in our heart and mind. We all are not artists, architects, musicians or storytellers but we live vicariously (experience through someone else by using the power of our imagination) just as if it has happened to us. We buy the music, books, and go to movies that reflect what appeals to us and say what we think and believe. We imagine ourselves in situations and places, that only art and music can take us. Culture is what produces the art and the music and therefore controls the dreams and aspirations of the people.

Our God is the creator of all things, even our ability to be creative. There is not anything made that He did not create first in the spiritual realm. Everything that is created in His Kingdom is noble, just, pure, lovely, of good report, virtuous and praiseworthy. These things lift our souls and spirits high and bring us joy, peace and the abundant life.

The Bible is our standard for literature. The Bible opens our heart and our mind to things way beyond the capabilities of our humanness. Within its pages, the emotions of the heart come to life, all the wonders of science ignite our imagination and we see the power of the universe enacted right before our eyes as people are healed, demons are cast out and the dead are raised.

Community

In order to tie the purpose of culture together, we need to look at the concept of community. Culture is what makes community work. One would think that if everyone has the same culture there would be total unity. This would be true; however, not everyone accepts in totality-the whole culture.

The goal for both the Church and family is community. God's grand plan is for us to rule and reign with His Son over this earth. He instructs us to have the mind of Christ: that means having the Wisdom of God. Culture reveals the wisdom of God. Wisdom, when applied, will solve all our human problems, explains the love of God, reveals the rewards of obedience, gives understanding of the laws of the universe, shows how to maintain relationships, and makes clear how to attract and conduct ourselves in the presence of God. Kingdom Culture is the vehicle that brings about community and community is the vehicle that communicates the wisdom of God to the world.

It is only when we have a Kingdom mind-set will we be able to work toward community. In the 1st century, knowledge of citizenship in the Kingdom was fundamental and therefore anyone who was "born again" was a part of the church community. When people were added to the Lord, they were added to the Church. When they belonged to Christ, they belonged equally to His body.

This early Church was bound, one to another by a covenant, a covenant of Love. Their love was translated into commitment. This commitment was their obligation to service and self-sacrifice. Community was possible because they were able to overlook one another's faults and shortcomings. Their commitment was directed to the spiritual growth of one another.

The Community that they enjoyed together, allowed spiritual growth to take place. When there is mutual respect for others, an atmosphere abounds where the Spirit of God can bring about the forming of Christ in His body. The Kingdom Culture of the Church is what the world still needs to witness. The world, however, can never realize its desire for community because it will not accept Kingdom culture.

We cannot superimpose Kingdom Culture on top of world culture and call it Christian. There is an absolute difference between the two. We cannot bring the world into the Church nor can we take the Church into the world. The two are separate. The cultures are diametrically opposed to each other.

From Paul's first letter to the Corinthians, we note that the severest punishment for a believer who committed a gross sin was to be excluded from the Church. These early Christians looked to the Church for strength as they belonged to one another. To be left out of the community meant coming out from underneath the umbrella of fellowship.

The early Church had all things in common. This is most often thought of only in regards to the distribution of wealth. The distribution of wealth was a direct result of their culture. Nevertheless, the context that brought about this act of generosity is much broader than this because there was a greater dynamic going on then the surrendering of one's possessions.

The people assembled there had ALL things in common. This meant that their faith was common. Their love for one another was common. Their values and strength of character was common. Their worship and service to their God and King was common. What they had was common-unity-COMMUNITY.

34

Chapter Five

Kingdom Government

Fundamentals of Government

In Chapter four, we discussed the seven major elements of Kingdom Culture. That which is of primary importance, however, is Government. It is from the seat of power or the throne that the other six find their shape and form.

As we look closer, we find that there are nine fundamental branches that make up the tree of Government. The tasks performed by those involved are vital to the orderly operation of a nation.

I. Constitution and Laws

A major concern for any government is its relationship with its citizens. This relationship is spelled out in some form of Constitution along with its Laws. This is even more paramount in the Kingdom of God because, as we said from the beginning, it is all about Relationship.

God knew that man's rebellion against His rule would put him under the rule of Satan. His heart would be changed from a heart that had affection toward God to a heart of stone. Instead of having a heart of "giving", he would now possess a heart of "getting". His new heart would cause him to put himself first (self-centeredness) before all others and the passions of his perverted soul would dominate him throughout his life.

When God was ready to reveal to the whole world His Grand Plan, He chose a people who would embrace His promise by entering into a covenant with Him. Therefore, He miraculously brought them out of bondage from the Egyptians and in bringing them out, He formed them into a nation of people and He himself became their King. They were not a kingdom at that time because; at the beginning they had no territory. God, however, did give to them a promise of land that would be theirs forever.

Kingdom Government

To show His great love for them and to reveal to them that He was indeed their King, God entered into another covenant with them. Their part of the covenant was to keep the laws that were given to them through Moses. These laws, when obeyed, would allow peace and harmony to exist and would bring forth a blessing and not a curse to those within the Kingdom that God was establishing in the Promised Land.

The covenant, with its terms and conditions, became their constitution (the document outlining the laws and principles by which they were to be governed). God put His wisdom of government into a book (we now call it The Bible) that was to be read and explained to each generation so that each citizen could know their God (king) and understand their responsibility as citizens.

The laws that Moses brought down from the mountain and the subsequent laws that were written down in the Torah, pertained to every area of life. The laws, when obeyed, revealed the love, compassion, wisdom, and the power of their God Jehovah. Their obedience to the Laws brought blessings to the people and showed the kingdoms of the world the greatness (power and wisdom) of Israel's God.

Laws were instituted for their good; not to limit their freedom but enable them to enjoy life and have it more abundantly. When God's laws were broken; suffering, sickness and pain were the result. This was not a result of God's anger because of their breaking the covenant, but just the normal consequences of their behavior. It was when they rebelled and set up other gods to worship that the finger of God came down to punish them.

There were also dietary and sanitation laws that protected the people from disease. When they were not followed, sickness and even death resulted. Obedience resulted in health and safety for all.

A Present Day story

I am presently working on a project for a village in the mountains of Haiti. There is no electricity, no running water and no toilet facilities. The local pastor has been preaching the

Gospel of Jesus Christ for 22 years and over 500 souls have come to Christ. I am working with them and sharing the Gospel of the Kingdom,

This is a primitive society where no government influence is present for the good of the people. Here, this local Church has the opportunity to extend the culture of the Kingdom by obeying the laws in the Old Testament that pertain to sanitation, diet, water, and even marital relationships, as AIDS and TB is so out of control.

Just as the nation of Israel was to make the name of their God known to the whole World, this Haitian mountain Church can make His name known to the 10,000 people that live in that area. Others will know that obeying the Lord and His laws not only brings freedom from guilt and shame BUT also blessings that come through OBEDIENCE. By showing that they obey the King and are blessed because of it, the whole mountain area will see the love, compassion, mercy, grace and power of their God.

II. Taxation

Our covenant with an invisible God is first spiritual and then becomes physical, so taxation is first spiritual and then becomes physical. Therefore, taxation in the spiritual realm is known as the tithe.

There are certain components of a kingdom that are best done by the King and his government. These areas are functions that are not for one person or family but are for the good and benefit of all those in the kingdom. These include roads, a water system, defense, commerce, and other areas that develop as a society enters the technological age.

In order for the citizens to take some responsibility for their own welfare, the King taxes the people and spends the proceeds accordingly. A good king does not need to ask the citizenry for permission to do what he thinks best. Here is a parallel thought; our children do not ask; the parents just do what they think or know what is best for the whole family.

Tithing is much more than just giving money to the Church. Tithing is the signifying of our approval of the way our King is

37

benefiting us through the services He is providing. We are showing our gratitude and thanksgiving though our obedience. It is showing our allegiance and loyalty to the King.

When we gladly bring our tithes to the Church, which is His governing influence here on earth, God makes His provisions available to us and rebukes the devourer for us.

When we do this collectively and when it becomes a part of our culture, the other nations will call us blessed because they will see the goodness of our God.

It is important to note that the tithe is 10%: that is for everyone; it is not progressive. The payment of the tithe is for the poor as well as the rich. The Churches that do not teach tithing as an element of being a responsible citizen of the kingdom, do their people a great disservice and bring upon them great harm and pain. The judgment that will come upon them will be severe because Christ's Church is to be a light and salt in the earth that they might reveal the real King to the other nations.

III. Security/Protection – Expansion

A king builds an army to protect that which is His. He defends His territory against all invaders, whether physical, psychological or spiritual. He is just as protective over the work ethic, talents and abilities of his citizens. These resources reveal His wealth and enable His citizens to carry on commerce and trade with other nations. A king does not willingly give these up without a fight.

When a king has a powerful army, His citizens are secure in knowing that when they are under His rule, there is safety. A king not only provides for national defense but also make provision for individual citizens to defend themselves against personal attack that would destroy their desire to be a part of Kingdom Culture.

Our King Jesus knows that we wrestle not against flesh and blood but against principalities, against the powers, against world rulers of this present darkness, and against hosts of wickedness in heavenly places. He therefore has given us the needed armor to, not only protect ourselves but to go on the offensive. He promises that He will never leave us nor forsake us. He promises victory in the fight.

Some kings just want to hold on to what they have. Our King however, has a mission to take back what was stolen from His Father when man gave away the keys to the kingdom through deceit and a promise of freedom from the control of God.

Jesus is therefore gathering the "called out ones" to be a citizen's army. After Jesus described the character of the citizens of the kingdom, He tells says that they are to be salt and light. There are to keep safe the culture they enjoy and to extend their culture to others as well.

The army of God is not to just to hang on to the gains it has made but also to extend the king's kingdom through the pulling down of strongholds and attacking the enemy wherever he rears his ugly head. Just as light is not to be hid, His kingdom, its culture, is not to be hid inside the four walls of a local church. We are to take the battle to the streets and let the His light shine.

IV. Justice

Life without justice is a life of torment in a kingdom for those that are righteous. The wrong doer must be punished and righteousness upheld. Justice makes the terms—right and wrong—meaningful. Justice knows no skin color, gender or religion. Justice is not negotiable.

Even though it may seem as if the ungodly are not punished, our King Jesus lets us know that all will be judged, the ungodly for their rebellion and the godly for their works of righteousness. At the end of life, there is justice for all. In the spiritual and the physical alike; what we sow, we shall also reap.

Kingdom Culture must reveal this aspect of life. It is what the world desperately needs and longs for. They see the injustice of those that have their own personal agendas. They see the immorality of those that we once admired. They see the poor, elderly, the less intelligent taken advantage of, and no one to take up their cause for justice.

Kingdom justice teaches us that each one of us is RESPONSIBLE for our own deeds. We are held ACCOUNTABLE to others for our behavior. Justice is for ALL-no one is above being judged. The Bible is our standard for justice.

Our Kingdom Culture demands that we must take a stand against injustice. If each local, individual sovereign church is promoting its own culture by staying silent, then Kingdom Culture has no voice. Today, so many pastors are remaining silent when the cry for justice would give the Holy Spirit an opportunity to speak to the ungodly and bring conviction of sin, righteousness and judgment.

V. Commerce

Commerce deals with the exchange of goods and services, from the producer to the final consumer. It encompasses the trading of something of economic value such as goods, services, information, or money between two or more entities.

Commerce in Kingdom Culture means there is an exchange of something of value. In the Kingdom of God, that which has the most value is FAITH. The buyer has faith that the product or service is of the quality desired and will meet their needs. The seller has faith that the money or promise of payment will meet the cost of production and make him a profit. Commerce in Kingdom Culture is founded on honesty and righteousness between two people.

Integrity is the bedrock of commerce in God's Kingdom and must be a part of the culture that we reveal to the world by the Church and Family. The world revolves around commerce. Even each individual finds fulfillment in the exchange of what he has to offer (his talents and abilities) for something that he finds important. Commerce in the kingdom is a part of experiencing the Abundant Life.

Closely related to commerce is the economic system of a culture. As citizens of the Kingdom of heaven, we are involved in the two different economic systems. The world's culture operates on a medium of exchange or currency: money. Kingdom Culture operates on a medium of exchange, which is FAITH.

VI. Education

Much of the present day dilemma in our American society is the result of the Church allowing culture to be taught at the discretion of the arm of government known as the public schools system. The public schools are guiding the morals, attitudes, knowledge, and decision-making of eighty-nine percent of our children instead of the Church.

As a result, when our children go to the Universities, the godless culture learned in grade school is reinforced and even expanded upon. These graduates then go on to be the business leaders, schoolteachers, mothers, and fathers of our grand children. Is it any wonder that the ball of godlessness keeps on rolling?

Satan has deceived the church once again in order that he can keep his kingdom safe from being over-taken by the Kingdom of God. Satan will do whatever it takes to keep the light from shining into the darkness of his kingdom and to make sure our salt has lost its saltiness.

The National Education Association in 1951 proclaimed, "It is important that people who are to live and work together shall have a common mind, a like heritage of purpose, religious ideals, love of country, duty, and wisdom to guide and inspire them."[1] The message of their civics handbook was fortified with selections from Old and New Testament passages, the Ten Commandments, the Lord's Prayer, the Golden Rule, the Boy Scout Oath, and patriotic songs. Because it looked good on the outside, the Church bought into it and handed the formulation of our children's worldview over to the godless. We were deceived.

Gone are the Sunday School classes of the 40's and 50's. Gone are the Sunday night and Wednesday night services to teach the saints the Word of God regarding - the necessity for and the opportunity for corporate prayer. Gone are the Levites of Ezra's day that made sure every man, woman and child understood the Word after the reading of the Law. (See Nehemiah 8:7-8).

Education is the responsibility of the family and is reinforced by the Church. Education is more than reading, writing and arithmetic; it is the means of formation of the whole person.

Because parents have lost their own way in this godless world, our children have no moral compass to look to in order that they maintain their true north heading.

VII.   Covenants

To insure the continuation of the present government for future generations, those taking office take an oath of allegiance saying that they will uphold (support and defend) the constitution and laws of the Land. These oaths are important because the one taking the oath possess authority and power to direct and lead.

"The secret of the Lord is with those that fear Him, and He will show them His covenants." (Ps.25:14). The oath is similar to a covenant but without the penalties associated with breaking a contract. However, an oath speaks volumes of the integrity of the one giving the oath. God has made many oaths and with all, He was and is found faithful; even when the Nation of Israel deserved to be destroyed God kept His oath. An oath cannot be altered or changed; it is permanent.

In others words, the one who made the oath must keep it regardless of circumstances. James gives us fair warning regarding making an oath when he writes in James 5:12, *"But above all, my brethren, do not swear, either by heaven or by earth or with any other oath. But let your "Yes" be "Yes," and your "No," "No," lest you fall into judgment."*

A covenant is different in that it is the joining of two or more people into a binding relationship. It could be a pact between equals: brothers, friends, marriage, or between neighbors. It also could be a pact between unequals: stronger/weaker, superior/inferior. It could be between nations but it also could be between individuals. It is usually the weaker who initiates the agreement by coming to the stronger or it could be the stronger imposing his agreement upon the weaker; in either case, the stronger dictates the terms and conditions of the agreement.

In regards to our covenant with God, it is a covenant between UNEQUALS. What is so unique about our covenant is that the Stronger has come to make a covenant with the weaker. It is His desire to have a relationship with the lesser: the Holy with the

Sinner. We did not choose to come to Him to appease His Anger or to seek His blessing. He comes to us and offers Himself to be our *protector*, our *provider*, and our *friend*. He comes to us and offers forgiveness in order that He might have a relationship. He comes to us and reveals Himself as our Father, not just our Creator.

God has a purpose for His creation. He created man to have dominion over His Kingdom therefore He offers man a covenant that allows him come back and resume his purpose.

God has sealed this covenant, first with an oath and then with the blood of His only begotten Son. God is faithful to keep His part of the agreement. The question remains: will we keep ours?

The agreement between God and man is not one-side therefore, we must understand the terms and conditions, as well as the blessings and the penalties.

1. Covenants consist of terms, conditions, and promises of the agreement.
2 There is an oath signifying both individuals will keep the terms of the agreement.
3. There is a curse (penalty) for each one, should they break the agreement.
4. There is a sealing of the covenant by some external act such as the blood sacrifice (signature).

In Exodus 19:3-6 God gives Moses a promise: *"Now therefore, if you will indeed obey My voice and keep My covenant, then you shall be a special treasure to Me above all people; for all the earth is Mine. And you shall be to Me a kingdom of priests and a holy nation."*

Notice that the Promise is tied with a condition. This is the condition: if the children of Israel obey God's voice and keep His covenant, God will keep His Promise. God has much at stake here. He is looking way beyond the Nation of Israel. He expects Israel to separate itself from other nations because of their special relationship with Him. They were to be a holy people because He is Holy. It would be, because of their separation, having a culture entirely different from other nations, that these other nations would learn of the living God.

Kingdom Government

In Exodus 20, God begins to put down the conditions that they must follow and gives Moses the Ten Commandments to give to the people. In Exodus 24:3 and 7, the people made a solemn oath of obedience to follow the Lord.

In addition to keeping the Ten Commandments they were required to offer animal sacrifices. These sacrifices were a reminder that justice must be served in order for God to forgive their sin. The sacrifices were gifts given to show honor to God. The sacrifices were a indication of their desire for intimancy, their confession of sin and desire for pardon. The sacrifices were offered in a spirit of faith, following the example of Abraham when he offered Issac. The sacrifices offered were the lambs without blemish, the first fruits and others. The point to be made is that they were costly to those making the offering.

The Nation of Israel did not escape the penalties for breaking the covenant. The Curses found in Deuteronomy 28 were harsh and terrible. It was not until the Nation of Israel repented and called upon God that they found deliverance and rest.

God's covenant with us is our guarantee that every promise He has given to us will be fulfilled. It is the Title deed to our inheritance. If we are thinking from a Man-Centered Worldview, we might be thinking of earthly blessings such as heaven, prosperity, health, deliverance from evil situations. If we are thinking from a Kingdom Worldview, we are thinking of strength to live a holy life, escape from temptation, being filled His righteousness, abounding in peace, love and joy, growing in the grace of God, and maturing into Sonship.

When we instruct people to ACCEPT Jesus as our Savor, what does that mean? What does that mean to those that come forward to the Alters in our churches or at our dining room table?

Do they understand that they are entering into a relationship that must be developed and are not just being a part of a different religion? Do they realize that God will not allow them to mix their former religion with their relationship with Him?

Do they understand that they are entering into a covenant relationship that has penalties if not adhered to? Do they understand they must "die to self" in order for them to fulfill their part of the agreement?

The covenant that God offers us is a blood covenant. God's son shed His blood, but He calls us to offer our bodies as a living sacrifice. God has made all the arrangements for the execution of the covenant. All we need to do is trust in Him and love Him.

VIII.   Citizenship

From the beginning of this book, we have learned, 'It is all about relationship'. It still is about relationship but we now need to consider what our relationship with the King additionally means to us. What we are now talking about, of course, is our life as a citizen of the Kingdom. It is not a matter of living according to laws, creeds, or identifying with some doctrine of faith. Too often the message of the Kingdom has been turned from a life-giving source into a religion that has no power. Even the name, "Christian" has become a religious term whose adherents have no concept of the Kingdom of God, the joys of citizenship or the privileges of living under a new government.

"Now therefore you are no more strangers and foreigners, but fellow citizens with the saints, and members of the household of God; having been built on the foundation of the apostles and prophets, Jesus Christ Himself being the chief cornerstone; In whom the whole building, being fitted together, grows into a holy temple in the Lord: in whom you also are built together for a dwelling place of God in the Spirit." (Eph. 2:19-22).

Consider the following Scriptures relating to the visible and the invisible:

- *For since the creation of the world His invisible attributes are clearly seen, being understood by the things that are made, even His eternal power and Godhead, so that they are without excuse,* (Rom. 1:19-20)

- *By faith we understand that the worlds were framed by the word of God, so that the things which are seen were not made of things which are visible.* (Heb 11:3)

- *For by Him all things were created that are in heaven and that are on earth, visible and invisible, whether thrones or*

> *dominions or principalities or powers. All things were created through Him and for Him.* (Col. 1:15-17)

This last verse is of particular interest to us as it mentions thrones, dominions, principalities and powers. They were created in the invisible as well as in the visible. They are in the unseen as well as in the seen. Kingdoms are in the invisible realm and in the visible realm.

Citizenship has no meaning outside a governmental setting. Just as citizens of dictatorships have no say as to how their lives are governed; those in the kingdom of darkness are slaves to Satan and have no say so in how they are governed.

We, however, are people with liberty. We are no longer slaves of unrighteousness but can choose this day who we will serve. We are free to live by Faith.

A kingdom has a king and it has citizens. The citizens have rights and privileges because they are in a convent relationship with the king. This is a legal and binding relationship with responsibilities on both parties. The Apostle Paul made mentioned that he was a Roman citizen by birth while others had received their citizenship through purchase. Because he was a citizen, he enjoyed certain privileges. (See John 1:12-13 & Philippians 3:20-21).

Just because we are citizens of the USA does not automatically give us the right to act as an Ambassador. Ambassadors are appointed and therefore cannot, by their own accord, place themselves in that position. Just as importantly, when they are appointed, they are committed to their governments interests and do not speak on their own behave.

Let us look at the relationship that Jesus had with His Father

- *Jesus said to them, "My Father is always at his work to this very day, and I, too, am working."* (John 5:17, NIV)

- *Jesus gave them this answer: "I tell you the truth, the Son can do nothing by himself; he can do only what he sees his Father doing, because whatever the Father does the Son also does.* (John 5:17)

- *By myself I can do nothing; I judge only as I hear, and my judgment is just, for I seek not to please myself but him who sent me.* (John 5:30, NIV)

- *For I have not spoken on My own authority; but the Father who sent Me gave Me a command, what I should say and what I should speak. And I know that His command is everlasting life. Therefore, whatever I speak, just as the Father has told Me, so I speak."* (John 12:49-50)

If I am related to the King, does that automatically give to me kingdom powers? No, but it does make possible for the King to confer upon me special powers to act on his behave as He would delegate.

IX. Health

A healthy nation is a prosperous nation. Sick people cannot work to the best of their ability and contribute to the wealth of the nation. It is not just a matter of economics that moves the King to provide healing, but it is also a matter of love for those in His kingdom.

It is part of His nature to provide wholeness in body and mind as well as spirit to His people. It is not just because we are God's children that He makes healing available but it is because we are citizens of His Kingdom.

God has made a covenant with the Believer and as part of His family; we are entitled to His care and provision. Just as our earthly father watches over our health and provides for us; God does the same for the Believer.

King David tells of the blessings of being connected with God's Kingdom, "Ps 103:2-5, *"Bless the Lord, O my soul, and forget not all His benefits: "Who forgives all your iniquities, who heals all your diseases, who redeems your life from destruction, who crowns you with loving-kindness and tender mercies, who satisfies your mouth with good things, so that your youth is renewed like the eagles."*

In the story found in 2 Kings: 5:1-14, Naaman, a beloved general who had contacted leprosy, goes to his master, the King of Syria, who then sends a letter to the King of Israel. When the King of Israel got the letter, he tore his clothes and said, *"Am I*

47

God, to kill and make alive, that this man sends a man to me to heal him of his leprosy?"

The widespread idea was that, since the King of Israel gave out blessings and since healing was in the land of Israel, it must be also given out by the king. The problem with this thinking was that they were looking to the wrong King. It was the King of Heaven, the true ruler of the Nation of Israel, which provided the healing.

Yes, healing is provided to the citizens; however, even the citizens can receive healing only when two things are present: Trust and Obedience. Both of these are included in principle of Faith. Trust is a matter of relationship. If you or I trust someone, it is because we believe we know his or her heart or motive. God has no other motive than to show His love for you. Obedience is a result of knowing the Will and the power of the one we are approaching with our request and acting accordingly.

Under the old covenant, God's people were healed when they believed what God said, and then acted on it. Under the new covenant, based on the life, death and resurrection of Jesus, we have even better promises. Jesus fulfilled God's Word and now we have faith that by His stripes we are healed.

---

[1] Eagle Forum: "The Phyllis Schlafly Report", Volume 39 #1, 2005, Follies and Failures of the National Education Assn.

Chapter Six

The Kingdom Established

Starting at the Beginning

We are on a journey that leads to God's final purpose for humanity. This journey will take us from the establishment of the Kingdom of God at creation until Jesus turns everything over to His Father. A lot transpires in between these two events, so it is important that we have a correct starting point.

If we are going to have an understanding of life that allows us to live it to its fullest, we must have a perspective of the whole that sees the very beginning as well as the ending. For this to happen we must begin at the correct starting point and that can only be with God Himself before creation. As with any design, the starting point is within the creator, within his heart and mind. We must begin with God and see life with a Kingdom mind-set.

We believe in ONE God who reveals Himself as Father, Son, and Holy Spirit. They are equal in all things but with different responsibilities to perform. The overpowering character quality of our Triune God is LOVE and it is out of this LOVE that the unity of the Godhead is seen working together to create the heavens and the Earth. The Father speaks, the Son is the Word spoken and the Spirit (the Spirit of the Father) takes that which the Father speaks and gives it shape and form.

The paternal heart of the Father reveals itself in the creation of the Kingdom of God on earth. It is within this earthly Kingdom that the Father will accomplish four major objectives: *First*, to extend His kingdom from the invisible to the visible and *Secondly*, to make known the fullness of His Being, His full personality. *Thirdly*, His objective is to provide a body of believers for his Son in order that we may share His nature as His children and contribute in the rule of the Kingdom. *Lastly*, it is to provide a temple for the Holy Spirit.

God has a Dream

When an entrepreneur thinks he/she knows enough about something and believes it has great value, something stirs within him that can cause him to have an idea that maybe others could benefit from his knowledge and experience. Once he has an idea, he lets it incubate until a dream is formed and then his creative juices begin to flow. He first sees it as a big puzzle and then he slowly begins to fit all the pieces together. As the pieces come together, he begins to see the picture of something that could be. His dream begins to take shape and form and soon, he has a vision.

Once he has a vision there is no stopping him. The vision spurs him on to look for all that he needs to make that vision a reality. He knows he cannot do it alone so he shares his vision with others in hope they too will capture the vision and join him in the process of making it come into being; to give that dream and vision life.

He then begins to write a Mission Statement that outlines his rationale for going into business. It brings into the light his values, his philosophy of doing business and treatment of his employees. He writes his business plan so that he can share with others that he does not plan to fail but to succeed. He communicates his vision with exact detail revealing what he is going to create and then draws it or builds a model or a pattern of what he has in mind.

Isn't this exactly what God the Father did? He already has a Kingdom in the spiritual realm but He has a dream of extending his Kingdom to the visual or physical realm. The Father cannot do it alone so He discusses it with himself (His Word) (also known as self-talk) and with His Spirit. He starts with a conception of that which He is going to create in His mind, in His thoughts.

Regarding earth's kingdom, it is within God first unseen before it was produced (seen) even in the spiritual realm. He patterned it after His Kingdom in Heaven and since He cannot change, He must govern this new kingdom in the same fashion using the same righteous standards.

He has a dream of an extended Kingdom that is created in the physical realm with Man having dominion over all His creation. When all his thoughts and plans were finalized He spoke the Words and the Holy Spirit brought it into existence.

Colonization – Up until recently, schooling in the United States always consisted of World History and American History. Students of my generation were proud to be Americans because we learned of the hardships, struggles and sacrifices that our ancestors endured in order that we might have the society and the life that Americans have enjoyed over the last 200 years.

However, America was not always a sovereign nation. We first were a colony of Great Britain. Great Britain had established a commonwealth of nations and America was destined, at least in their minds, to be a part of that commonwealth. The term Commonwealth originally meant, a state or nation-state governed for the common good as opposed to an authoritarian state governed for the benefit of a given class of owners. Great Britain therefore, set out to colonize the new land that was discovered and make it part of their commonwealth.

Other nations also wanted a piece of this land that held so much promise. The Spanish, the French, and others wanted to lay claim to America in order to obtain a share of the great riches that this land had to offer.

The point to be noted is this; before Great Britain started its Colonization there existed no known governmental entity in this great land of ours (except the American Indians). Because it was 'Vacant Land', Great Britain sent people here to incorporate it into their commonwealth. Once a colony had been established, they sent governors to represent the King and an army to insure that this new colony would grow and prosper for the benefit of the commonwealth.

They set up a form of government that gave them control over all things produced, mined, or otherwise created wealth. They instituted laws, taxes, educational programs, and administrators over water, health and others areas needed for a functioning society. They also influenced this new land with their culture.

51

The Kingdom Established

Our founding fathers' would have been content to let the King of England rule if he had not tried to take advantage of the fledging colony. When the settlers finally had had enough, they revolted and the United States of America was formed. How did they set up their government? They did not reinvent the wheel regarding governing entirely. They realized that even though they did not want a king to rule over them, they knew they still needed a form of government that would unite the thirteen colonies under one flag, one rule of law that would guarantee the rights of its citizens and a central army whereby they could defend themselves.

They set in place a form of government called a *Republic*. A republic is a form of government in which the head of state is not a monarch and the citizens have an impact on their government. The word 'republic' is derived from the Latin phrase "res publica", which can be translated as "a public affair".[1]

The educational system, of this new republic, used the Bible as their textbook and their national motto was, "One nation under God". The preachers were the watchdogs over what would constitute right and wrong in this ever-growing nation. These preachers, representing God, would preach against the evils of the day until they were silenced or change had occurred. Their preaching affected individuals, families, businesses, education, and government. They, in reality, were like the Old Testament Prophets who made known the Word of God when the people and their kings strayed or departed from the LAW.

The Lord's Prayer – During what we call the Sermon on the Mount, Jesus addresses the crowd and tells them plainly that He is the Son of God. He does so by addressing God as "Our Father" in what we call, The Lord's Prayer. He means to emphasis the fact that His Father is in Heaven and as such, He is to be worshipped. Jesus then begins his prayer and the first thing that He asks is for the Father's Kingdom to come and His will to be done here on earth as it is in Heaven.

Jesus wanted the government of His Father's kingdom to return to earth. When His Father's Kingdom was ruling the earth, there was no sickness, no poverty, no pain, and no death. Jesus asks for the provision to be granted to his disciples and for forgiveness to be sought and for the Father to keep them from temptation in order that his disciples would be able to exercise authority over Satan and his demons. The Kingdom of God was the true Kingdom or government of the earth and one day His Kingdom will have power and the glory over the earth forever and forever.

The Creation of Man

We are made in God's Image – OT: Hebrew: demuwth (dem-ooth'); Spirit.

To be made in the *image* of another is to be made exactly like the original or have the same nature as the original. Image is hidden or invisible. It is the character of the original. We were made in the image of our Creator. We are to express His character or nature.

We are made after God's Likeness – OT: Hebrew: tselem (tseh'lem); Soul

To be made after the *likeness* of another is to behave in *the same* manner and express yourself in the same way. Likeness is outward; it is the behavior and actions that are seen. It is more than just being a loyal and faithful representative of God, he is to go about his assignment (operate and function) in the same manner as did His Creator.

IF GOD DID NOT CREATE THE EARTH, HE COULD NOT JUSTIFY CREATING MAN IN HIS IMAGE. WHY? GOD'S NATURE DEMANDS THAT HE EXERCISE DOMINION OVER ALL THAT HE POSSESSES. IF HE HAD CREATED MAN TO OCCUPY HEAVEN, HE COULD NOT HAVE MADE HIM IN HIS IMAGE BECAUSE GOD WILL NOT SHARE HIS GLORY WITH ANY OF THOSE HE HAS CREATED. THEREFORE, HE CREATED EARTH AND THEN MAN, THAT HE MIGHT HAVE DOMINION IN THE PHYSICAL REALM.

Before Adam rebelled, he was righteous and holy. He communed with His Creator and was faithful and obedient in all that he was given to do. He was given all the resources necessary to carry out his responsibilities of tending the garden and naming the animals. He was submissive to His Creator.

God said, "Let them have dominion". The, "them" refers to Adam and his wife and ALL their offspring. When God breathed life into man, there was, at that moment, a transfer of power. God delegates the responsibility, management and rule of His Kingdom to man. It is important that we understand the two terms used when God created man; image and likeness.

The Kingdom Connection-The Church

To understand the Importance of the Journey, you must first understand the Importance of the Kingdom.

It was from the Father's heart and in His infinite wisdom that He decided to create another kingdom to further His purposes. The first is spiritual, heavenly; the second is physical, earthly. In creating the heavens and the earth, God first created its territory and then its citizenry. God's vision was to retain his position as King over this new kingdom but give the citizens themselves, as His regents, dominion over all that He created. He called this new territory; earth. He called its citizens; man. So here, we have the essentials of a kingdom: a king, citizens and territory.

A kingdom is like the tree trunk. From the kingdom grows the branches or the culture that spreads out to cover the land. The fruit is the visible result of the culture of the tree. The tree's roots, grounded in soil, provide the nutrients that, in turn, determine the quality of the life of the tree and its fruit. The life of the tree, its roots, trunk, branches and fruit, all come from the seed. The fruit, however, is more than an expression of the culture; it contains the seed that makes possible for it to reproduce itself.

If we look at the fruit of a tree, we can ascertain the heart or the makeup of the tree itself. If we look to the attitudes and behaviors of the citizens of a nation, we can ascertain the heart or the seven elements that make up its culture.

The Church also is like unto a tree.

Jesus said, The Kingdom of God is within you. His Church is the "called-out ones" from the world. It is the collective body of Christ throughout the world. It is the whole company of the redeemed, the professing Believers. Therefore, the trunk represents the Church and the Kingdom of God, the branches represent its culture and the fruit represent the expression of that culture.

The Church is not to be the local expression of the Baptists, Catholics, Assemblies of God, or the Independents. THE CHURCH IS TO BE THE LOCAL EXPRESSION OF THE CULTURE OF THE KINGDOM OF GOD AND ITS KING, JESUS CHRIST.

When the local Church embraces the Kingdom of God and has a Kingdom Worldview, a culture grows and produces fruit for the rest of the world to see and to taste "that it is good". Within the fruit comes a seed to plant another tree (local church). So from the seed of one tree comes another tree and then another and then another. Soon an orchard is providing fruit for a nation.

Our journey is not just for us to enjoy but it is that we might understand God's purpose and therefore have an influence on our world. Our world is looking for the Kingdom of God and we have the responsibility to reveal it to them.

We find a parallel is the USA. Peoples from all over the world saw America as the land of opportunity. They saw America as the land of freedom and liberty to pursue happiness and fulfillment. When the world sees the liberty, peace and love in the Kingdom of God they will leave all behind to come into it just as people left all behind in their native counties to come to the USA.

Jesus said, *"I do not pray for these alone, but also for those who will believe in Me through their word..."* John 17:20

---

[1] http://en.wikipedia.org/wik/Republic

Chapter Seven

The Kingdom Lost

The Beginning of Rebellion

God had given them one command; *"Of every tree of the garden you may freely eat; but of the tree of the knowledge of good and evil you shall not eat, for in the day that you eat of it you shall surely die. Gen 2:17.* God had given them a conscience and a free will but Satan blinded their spiritual eyes to see the consequences to what they were about to do.

Adam had given the snake its name and found nothing in it or in the garden that would hurt him or cause him or his wife any harm. So when the snake spoke to Eve, she did not become alarmed or afraid, even though it was unusual for a snake or an animal to speak. Even though Adam and Eve enjoyed perfect communion with the Father, they allowed a snake to deceive them.

Obedience was the key to blessing for Adam and Eve and it is still that way for us today. When MAN rebelled, he lost the right to rule God's kingdom here on earth. Greater still, he lost more than dominion; he lost everything. He lost his relationship with his creator, his freedom, his peace and he lost his fellowship with a loving God. He even lost his prosperity.

In order that we might fully understand how the Kingdom was lost, we have to go back before the creation of the heavens and the earth. We have to go back to eternity past and look into the Kingdom of Heaven. We need to see what happened there that would eventually have a direct effect on man's dominion of the earth.

The Bible itself gives us a picture of the Kingdom of Heaven: *"Your throne, O God, is forever and ever; a scepter of righteousness is the scepter of Your kingdom. You love righteousness and hate wickedness."* (Ps 45:6-7).

Jesus (the Word) created all things; therefore, Lucifer an angel is a created being even though the Bible says he was more beautiful (a gem among precious stones, Ezekiel. 28:13-17) than all the others. Lucifer had access to God's presence as the worship leader of Heaven, nevertheless, pride entered his heart and then Lucifer knew exactly what he wanted and how he was going to get it. Listen to the five "I will's" statements from Isaiah 14:12-15 that he proudly boast:

I will ascend into Heaven
I will exalt my throne
I will also sit on the mount
I will ascend above the heights of the clouds
I will be like the most High

Lucifer was determined to go after what only God the Creator possessed. What Satan did not understand is that: God will not share His Glory with anyone. Neither will He share His Kingdom with anyone except His only begotten Son and with those that will be joint heirs with Him.

Because of his deception, God changed His name from Lucifer to Satan and he was expelled from God's Kingdom in Heaven. The Word of God does not leave us ignorant of who Satan is and who he has become because of his deception of Adam and Eve. He has become the ruler of the kingdom he stole from God.

Satan's Plan to get a Kingdom

Satan's plan to obtain a kingdom was to deceive Mankind just as he had deceived the angels that had fallen with him. He would promise them that they would be like God themselves. He knew, from experience, that when humanity rebelled, God would have no choice but to expel them from the garden and from His presence just as God had expelled him.

Once done, he would take over as ruler and step number one would be complete; Satan would have a kingdom. Satan would organize his kingdom after the pattern in heaven. He would copy God's organizational structure. Satan seeks to copy everything that God has and everything He has done. Satan did not create anything; he has only copied God's work and then perverted it to his own use.

Satan organized his demons (fallen angels) just as God has organized his angels. We see in Colossians 1:16 the pattern as *God created all things, visible and invisible, whether thrones or dominions or principalities or powers.* The same again in Ephesians 6:12, we see that *we do not wrestle against flesh and blood but against; principalities, against powers, against the rulers of the darkness of this age, against spiritual hosts of wickedness in heavenly places.*

He and his demons will tempt, deceive, oppress and bring people into the bondage of fear so that they can control them and take away their freedom. Satan's kingdom is this world. His kingdom is a system of beliefs that are contrary to the Word of God. This world system involves art, music, politics, spiritual matters, science, philosophy and all other aspects of life contrived without God. We are born into this world.

Satan realizes that if he could deceive humanity into accepting a perverted view of what an acceptable worldview should be, he could prevent his kingdom from being destroyed. Without God's people holding up the light of truth, the world is deceived and millions of people will face the same fate as that of Satan and his demons.

Satan's plan is to obliterate the message of the Kingdom of God and replace it with a moral belief system; a system that puts man at the center instead of God. Satan leaves in enough truth to make it reasonable, but his substitute is full of corruption.

The Gospel that MUST be Preached

Is the Gospel to be preached only of salvation and a ticket to Heaven when we die? Is it just the absence of tears, pain, sin, peace, sorrow, worship, etc. that we are expecting when we are face to face with Jesus? When we get to the place on the "other side" are we just going to be singing and bowing down for an eternity; or is there more to the Gospel?

Jesus Himself said that unless you are "born again" you cannot see nor can you enter the kingdom of God. Is it possible, however, that the Church has preached this message at the exclusion of the message that Jesus preached? Throughout the Gospels, we read that JESUS WENT ABOUT PREACHING THE GOSPEL OF THE KINGDOM.

Does the Kingdom message include, you must be "born again"? Does it include deliverance, healing, peace, freedom and more? Yes, it does; it has to because this is what Jesus preached and demonstrated. Jesus is the door into the kingdom and there is no other way we can enter the kingdom except through faith in Him.

The message of the CROSS is followed by the message of the RESURRECTION. The message of the resurrection is followed by the message of Christ's ASCENSION. If we just hang out near the cross and the empty tomb, we lose understanding of the complete mission of Christ and the Father's grand plan for His creation.

WHEN WE ARE "BORN AGAIN", WE ARE NOT ONLY PLACED INTO THE FAMILY OF GOD, WE BECOME CITIZENS OF ANOTHER KINGDOM WITH ALL THE RIGHTS AND PRIVILEGES OF THIS KINGDOM. IT IS IMPORTANT THAT WE GET THIS RIGHT BECAUSE THIS IS THE REASON JESUS LEFT HEAVEN AND TOOK ON THE FORM OF MAN. HE ENDURED THE CROSS AND ACCEPTED THE SHAME FOR THE JOY THAT WOULD FOLLOW. WHAT IS THEN THE JOY TO FOLLOW? IT IS OUR BEING RESTORED INTO FELLOWSHIP WITH THE FATHER AND THEN BEING PLACED INTO A POSITION ENABLING US TO RULE WITH HIM.

Jesus was always talking to his disciples about entering, seeing, and inheriting the Kingdom prepared for God's children. He gave us something to live for Now as well as after death. Jesus gave us this prayer... *"Thy kingdom come, thy will be done, on earth as it is in heaven."* We are to influence this world, utterly, totally, completely. We are to occupy until He comes. We are to replace the lawless world system we are living in for a kingdom with Righteousness. We are to invade this world with the Gospel of the Kingdom and replace the world's culture with the culture of the Kingdom of God.

Jesus is determined to build a Church, a body of believers that would return His Father's Kingdom on the earth to its original state. To accomplish that goal God would have many sons and daughters working with him to turn the world right side up. To accomplish this, however, requires the complete revelation of Christ. First, there is the revelation of Christ as He comes to seek and to save those that are lost. Then we have the revelation of His joining forces with His Church to extend His kingdom as they do battle with the forces of darkness.

Jesus is the only door that leads into the kingdom. Without acknowledging this we cannot be "born again" nor enter the Kingdom. It is an indispensible step but it is not the entire journey. If we focus on this first step, we will never enjoy the many blessings that belong to God's children as we mature into Sonship and are made ready to reign with Jesus. God the Father is preparing us for something. He expects us to further His Kingdom here on earth. Everything God created has a purpose and only as it fulfills that purpose is GLORY revealed.

The Kingdom Understood

There is nothing more important to the Church today than a clear concise understanding of the Kingdom of God. Jesus called everyone to repentance: meaning to have a change in their thinking. Therefore, He spends much time explaining what is offered in place of what they are now holding on to. The Jews were holding on to a false idea of the Kingdom and obedience to the Law as the means to please God.

Given that our destiny is tied to the Kingdom of God, we must recognize six things that Satan does not want you to know:

- The Kingdom of God is available to you
- How to enter the Kingdom
- Once you enter the Kingdom, you are a citizen of the Kingdom
- The culture of the Kingdom
- Your authority in the Kingdom
- The Power that is available through the Baptism in the Holy Spirit as the King's representative

The language of the Kingdom of Heaven and the Kingdom of God are both used in the Gospels, therefore, the first thing that needs to be addressed is the question; is there a difference between these two terms. Both belong to the spiritual realm but there is a difference.

The Kingdom of Heaven is the sphere or jurisdiction where the Father rules over all creation, including the Heavenlies. His authority is exercised over his entire domain. It is here that His throne is established. Before the foundations of the earth and the heavens, Jesus existed as the Father's Word. There was only one throne and this was the governmental center in the spiritual realm where the Father executed judgment as well as mercy and grace over His Kingdom. All beings, whether Angels, Cherubs, Arch Angels, Seraphim and Cherubim, are subject to His demands and both His authority and power are absolute.

However, when His Word took on flesh and became a man, the Father started to rearrange the furniture in the throne room. Jesus was obedient to all that He was given to do (He took upon himself the sins of the whole world and paid the penalty of death to satisfy the judgment of God). Because of His obedience, the Father has given Him a name above of all names. When Jesus ascended into Heaven after being on the earth 40 days after His resurrection from the dead, God made Him His Lord and Christ and set Him upon His own throne from which He will judge the quick and the dead.

Jesus is subject to His father's authority and even though He rules as King of kings and Lord of lords, He too, does the will of the Father. When we talk about Jesus being King of kings, we are talking of governments. When we are talking about Jesus being Lord of lords we are talking of ownership of property.

The Kingdom of God is also a spiritual kingdom but there are two big differences. The first difference is the sphere of influence. The jurisdiction of the Kingdom of God is not in the heavenlies but in the hearts of men on the earth. The second difference is the person in the position of authority. Jesus is the King of Kings and His Father has given all authority to Him. Jesus is King but not all peoples of the earth are His subjects. His jurisdiction is restricted to those that are Citizens of the Kingdom; however, it is to the believers that He gives permission to use His authority to act as His ambassadors.

The Father sent His Word, clothed in flesh, and because we believe His Word, the Father has given us power to become His children. Throughout the Gospels, Jesus gave a clear picture of His Kingdom and what would be expected of the citizens of His Kingdom. The Father took us out from the kingdom of darkness and translated us into Kingdom of His Son. By His Spirit, we are "born again" and therefore He said that if we give ourselves as a living sacrifice, we would be transformed into the image of His Son. When completed, God's grand plan would be realized.

As citizens of the Kingdom of God, we are also citizens of the Kingdom of Heaven. I have never been to Heaven (except in the spirit-Heb 4:16) but I am very much a part of the Kingdom of Heaven as that is where my Father resides and has His throne. The authority that the Father gave to His Son, His son has given to us that we might go and extend His Kingdom – the Kingdom of God throughout the whole earth. This is our sphere of influence. Jesus has restored to us – dominion over the earth.

Chapter Eight

The Kingdom Reclaimed

God sets His plan into motion

Before God could fulfill His grand plan for us, He had to reclaim His Kingdom from the usurper, Satan himself. Satan had stolen His Kingdom from those God had personally put in charge to establish His rule here on earth. Therefore, God began His own spiritual warfare against Satan. This fight was between two kingdoms, between two governments.

So the Lord God said to the serpent, "This is your punishment: You are singled out from among all the domestic and wild animals of the whole earth-to be cursed. You shall gravel in the dust as long as you live, crawling along on your belly. From now on, you and the woman will be enemies, as will your offspring and hers. You will strike his heel, but he will crush your head."

The first part of this pronouncement God deals with the snake, who allowed himself to be used to deceive man. The serpent was subject to Adam because God had given Adam DOMINION over the creatures on the earth and the fishes of the sea. Therefore, by agreeing to be an instrument in the deception of Eve, a curse fell upon it. Whatever form it once occupied, the serpent is now to crawl upon its belly and swallow the dust of the earth.

He then turns His attention to Satan. Satan knew that God's grand plan is for man to have dominion over the earth. He knew also that as man grew in the knowledge of God's Word, he would mature and grow in the nature of God, bringing forth the Kingdom of Heaven to earth.

The Promise is in vague terms and has a quality of mystery and ambiguity, therefore it is difficult to understand or interpret. There are no particulars such as; mode of deliverance, the time it is to come, or the agency by which it is to come. This should not surprise us as the Bible is written to believers and requires revelation from the one who inspired men to write it, the Holy Spirit. It does not require a college education or high intelligence; it only requires a humble spirit that is alive to the voice of God.

God pronounced the curse to the serpent and gives the first prophecy of a deathblow to Satan's deceitfully acquired kingdom. God is declaring that He will provide a deliverer who will reclaim His kingdom. This God does in the hearing of Adam and Eve that they might know that they will be forgiven and it will provide them hope for the future. Their faith in the Promise will give them peace that surpasses all understanding. It is a short statement but speaks volumes.

The Promise

With this Promise, God is saying, "Even though Satan has achieved his first objective of acquiring a kingdom; my Son will in the end, destroy his kingdom. He will think he has won over the opposition when he provokes men to kill Jesus. However, Jesus will be resurrected and He will win the victory over death and the grave."

War is declared between the seed of Satan (the children of disobedience) and the seed of the woman (the children of God). The hope of the world is contained in this Promise; a Promise that a future descendant of Adam would again have dominion over the earth.

Everything that follows is a record of this war between Satan's warriors and God's men of faith. We hear of people like Enoch, Noah, Abraham and Sarah and the Patriarchs. Everything relates to this Promise of reclaiming the Kingdom that was lost. It was not man that was lost; it was his kingdom. Reclaim the kingdom and in the process, man will be restored to fellowship with God.

In this Promise, God's people would see the mercy and grace of their Creator. It is a mercy and grace of such magnitude that it restores man to a place of purpose and fulfillment. However, the only thing that would allow this Promise to be realized is a change in government.

Suppressive governments take away; steal all dignity and self-respect that is instinctive in each man. I saw for myself, in communist Poland and in Myanmar, that people living in Communists and Socialistic countries or under dictatorships of self-centered men know firsthand the horror of such action. They feel worthless and of no value, therefore their morals decline and their cultures decline with them.

Adam, because he had lived under the government of God, knew immediately what had happened when he rebelled. He saw the shift in rulership from a benevolent God to a ruthless dictator.

God, in order that man would know that He keeps His promise, entered into covenants that would bind the two of them together. Man could rely on God to fulfill His promise because a relationship was established.

God's Prophecies of Reclaiming His Kingdom

God kept His promise alive by raising up prophets to reveal His strategy. Here's the strategy: He would provide a Messiah who would be a future King whose kingdom would have no end. God gave the promise to Adam and it was passed on from individual to individual until God found a man and woman who had faith in the promise that would exceed their sight of old age and their inability to have children. This couple would be the root beginnings of a family of Hebrew children and later a nation. His name was Abraham and to him the promise became more specific because it was from his seed, that the promised Messiah would come and all the nations would be blessed.

So from that time forward, prophets were chosen from among men to proclaim that God would keep His Promise. Until the time of Christ's birth, God's strategy was to give to men more and more revelation as to who His Messiah would be. Let us look at some of these prophecies:

- *"For unto us a Child is born, Unto us a Son is given; And the government will be upon His shoulder. And His name will be called Wonderful, Counselor, Mighty God, Everlasting Father, Prince of Peace. Of the increase of His government and peace there will be no end, upon the throne of David and over His*

> *kingdom, to order it and establish it with judgment and justice from that time forward, even forever."* (Isa. 9:6-7)

- *"I was watching in the night visions, And behold, One like the Son of Man, Coming with the clouds of heaven! He came to the Ancient of Days, And they brought Him near before Him. Then to Him was given dominion, glory, and a kingdom that all peoples, nations, and languages should serve Him. His dominion is an everlasting dominion, which shall not pass away, And His kingdom the one which shall not be destroyed."* (Dan. 7:13-14)

The Promise Fulfilled

God reclaimed his Kingdom just as was prophesied 4000 years earlier. In the fullness of time, Jesus was born of a virgin and as promised re-established His Father's kingdom through His sinless life, veracious death on the cross, resurrection, and then finally His ascension unto the right hand of the Father. All Believers can now take full advantage of their new citizenship because Satan's power has been broken. The power of sin is broken although Satan's head is not crushed. This will take place after the battle of Armageddon.

Jesus was fulfilling the Promise given to Adam. The Father knew how He was going to reclaim His kingdom and the virgin birth of His Son was the beginning of that fulfillment. Since by one man sin came into the world, it is by one man that sin would be taken away. Jesus lived a sinless life before all the people, took upon himself the sin of all mankind, and bore the curse for all; that ALL may be set free. He made an open display of all his enemies and conquered the grave when the Father raised Him from the dead. When He accomplished all that He was given to do, He sat down at the right hand of His Father. When He fulfilled His purpose, our Father made him both his Lord and His Christ to sit upon His throne.

Along with reclaiming His Father's Kingdom, Jesus gives to His disciples New Life. He gives them power to become children of God and enjoy a personal relationship with Him. Jesus' resurrection began the re-establishment of the Kingdom of God, and the returning to man his place of dominion. Jesus destroyed the power of sin by paying the penalty of rebellion against His Father therefore man is now free to choose whom he will serve.

We can look at what Jesus has done but it is important to note why he did what he did. Paul writes in Galatians 4:4-5, *"But when the fullness of the time had come, God sent forth His Son, born of a woman, born under the law, to redeem those who were under the law, that we might receive the adoption as sons.* See more on this important subject of Adoption in Chapter 13

As a result of God reclaiming His Kingdom two major events took place. They are now part of Church doctrine and must be understood by all who go by the name of Christian: Redemption and Justification.

Redemption - Free to Serve God.

In the Old Testament, we have this beautiful picture of God intervening on behalf of the children of Israel. He raises up Moses to be a deliverer of His people and through him He performs signs and wonders that causes Pharaoh to let His people leave Egypt. By doing so, God is fulfilling His covenant that He made with Abraham 400 years earlier. This covenant detailed how the Nation of Israel was to be a people from which the Deliverer (from Satan's rule) would come. Therefore, in the same sense that the Egyptians had their hand heavy upon the people, sin had (and still has) its hand on the heart of Men.

This is the point to know and understand; God was not just bringing a people out of bondage but He was taking unto Himself a people. He says, *"I am Yahweh... I will free you from slavery... and I will take you for my people and I will be your God".* In virtue of the covenant, Israel becomes a "holy people", "consecrated to God".

We too have been redeemed. Our slavery was just as real as the Children of Israel's slavery under the hand of the Egyptians, only theirs was physical and ours was spiritual. God has freed us from the slavery of sin. He has freed us from the power that sin had in our life. Note: in the same manner that justice demanded a payment from the Egyptians (the death of their first-born), our Redemption also required a payment and that payment was the blood of Jesus Christ, God's first-born Son; *"for without the shedding of blood there is no remission of sin."* God chose us to be His

67

children just as He chose the Children of Israel to be His people. He chose us and desires for us to mature and become "sons" in the Kingdom of God.

As part of the Adamic race, man is under the dominion of Satan. All those born of women are children of disobedience and are influenced by his lies, deceit and desire to destroy all that is righteous in this world. But thanks be unto God, we have been delivered out of the kingdom of darkness and "translated" into the kingdom of the Son.

Jesus' purpose, mission, and desire was and is to return to God His creation clothed in righteousness; including man. To know that we are restored into His presence is the source of our joy. There is no greater outward expression of those that call themselves children of God then that of joy. No one else can have it and no one can steal it from us. It is spiritual in its making. It is ours because we are redeemed and in fellowship with our Creator.

Justification - Born Again and now Citizens

Every person wants to feel that he or she has importance and does not deserve condemnation. We all want to be justified in our thoughts, words and deeds. We all want to stand in the face of our accusers and be able to say, "I told you, it's OK what I did". We all want to declare our "righteousness. We feel justified when we can make our cause triumph over that of an opponent and make the justice of our case known. Here is a problem; God says our Righteousness is as filthy rags.

There is one word that characterizes the Kingdom of God: Righteousness. The scepter that is in the King's right hand is Righteousness. The foundation of God's throne is Righteousness and Justice. However, the one word that characterizes Satan's kingdom or the kingdoms of this world is the complete opposite and that word is lawlessness.

When we consider our ways, have a change in our thinking regarding our sinfulness and seek God for forgiveness, God declares us justified or that justice has been satisfied. We receive this "declaration" by faith.

So here is the **FIRST** aspect of Justification; When Satan comes to accuse us before our Father, we hold in our hand a statement from God that says that we are justified or that justice has been served.

SECONDLY, through Justification, we come boldly before the throne of God to receive mercy and grace in our time of need. Justification places man back into a position of "right standing", therefore, we can stand before God without the threat of punishment because we now stand before Him, clothed in the righteousness of Christ. It is in consideration of this word, Justification, that we understand the justice and the holiness of God.

This aspect of Justification is so important because we can now come before the throne, being clothed in the Righteousness of Christ, and make petitions before the Living God. In James 5:16 we have it written, *"The effective, fervent prayer of a righteous man avails much".* It is the righteous man that pleads for the souls of the lost, healing for the sick, and deliverance for those captive and receives answers.

When God's people embrace this aspect of Justification, God rejoices. It is in knowing that they are justified that cause His followers to go out into the fields and make His name known to the ungodly and bring Righteousness to the Earth. It is in so doing that God's people are involved in extending His Kingdom throughout the whole Earth.

The **THIRD** aspect is also important for us to consider. When the father (in Luke 15:11-32) saw his prodigal son return, his heart leaped for joy. The son who was lost is now found. He calls for a robe to be put on him, a ring to be put on his finger and sandals to be placed on his feet. The father was restoring his son to a place of importance in His kingdom as a citizen. Those that do not have a Kingdom mindset overlook this very important part of Justification. This restoration to our original position before God allows us to take up again our role of Regent for the King of Heaven.

The **FOURTH** aspect of Justification is - eradication of our sinful nature. The old saying for the meaning of Justification,

"Just as if we didn't sin" is true, old things have passed away and all things have become new. God takes away our stony heart and replaces it with a heart of flesh so that we may walk in His statutes and keep his judgments. Therefore, God is not ashamed to call us His people and He will be our God.

If we still have a sinful nature, how could God ever say to us, "be perfect for I am perfect" and "be holy for I am holy"? We can no longer hide behind those familiar sayings, "I am not perfect, just forgiven" or "I'm just a sinner saved by grace". God will not accept such frivolous concoctions of the flesh - to save the flesh.

However, herein lies the problem for the Believer; the flesh is still subject to the influence of evil. Within our flesh, there is no good thing. It is only as we put to death our flesh in all areas of our lives that the Holy Spirit can transform us into the very image of Jesus Christ.

There is **ANOTHER** aspect of Justification that comes with the free gift of righteousness. It is this: Since God has given us a new spirit, God does not deal with our spirit nature any longer as an enemy. He now deals with our flesh. The flesh is the recipient of Satan's offensive moves against us. When we sin, it is not because of our sinful nature; the heart of flesh replaced that. When we sin, it is through our flesh. That is why we don't have to be "Born Again" every time we sin. We just need to confess our sin, *"and He is faithful and just to forgive us our sins and cleanse us from all unrighteousness"*.

For this reason, we can also cast out devils from people. Devils do not inhabit our spirit but they can oppress our flesh. This is also the explanation as to why a spirit can oppress Christians and why we can cast them out.

In summary, Justification for God means that He now has a people who He can make ready to rule in His place and that He can precede with His Grand Plan for His creation. Justification for us means (1) we can stand before God without thoughts of wrath or judgment. (2) We can come boldly before His throne and make our petitions known and extend His Kingdom. (3) Our position as Regent or Ambassador is restored. (4) Our sinful nature is done away with. (5) Our flesh is now the problem and is the reason for

God's activity with us. Demons can oppress our flesh; however, we have authority over them.

The Pharisees of Jesus' day believed that if they obeyed God's Law they would be justified. In fact, if they could accomplish this, then they really would be justified. However, the Pharisees made an error in their understanding of the covenant. They separated the Law from the Promise where Faith is required.

Let us look at Justification as involving two kingdoms as we had done with Redemption. Jesus' purpose was and still is, to provide a way for man to be restored to the relationship he had with God and to restore righteousness to the Earth. His purpose also involves restoring Man back to the position that he had before Satan deceived him.

Man's position in the Garden of Eden was first spiritual before it was physical. Man received his authority, not from another man on earth, but from God, the ruler of His heavenly Kingdom. It was because of his relationship with the Creator of Earth that God gave him dominion over the Earth. He had both – Relationship and Position. When man rebelled against God, he lost both.

When Jesus invaded the realm of Satan, He came to conquer and destroy. By His death, resurrection and ascension He accomplished the reclaiming of His Father's kingdom. But this would be meaningless unless He also provided a way for Man to be restored to relationship and position in order to take dominion over the kingdom as God originally intended.

This He did by offering His blood as a payment of the penalty for sin. Secondly, He conquered the grave and destroyed the power of sin, sickness and disease that Satan had over us. When Jesus was promoted to King of the Kingdom of God, Man was restored to his place of dominion over the Earth.

Man, however, receives this justification by Faith. It is only by Faith that he is justified.

These two important truths of Redemption and Justification cannot be overlooked; or ignored. Every "Born Again" believer must understand these terms and have them imbedded in their heart and mind. These are spiritual truths and they can only be lived out in the believer by revelation that has comes by the Holy Spirit.

SALVATION INCORPORATES BOTH REDEMPTION AND JUSTIFICATION. IT IS THE WAY WE SEE HOW THEY FIT INTO OUR WORLDVIEW, HOWEVER, THAT DETERMINES WHETHER WE WILL HAVE A BIBLICAL MAN-CENTERED OR A KINGDOM WORLDVIEW.

Until Christians understand the full meaning of Redemption and Justification, they will never advance toward God's Grand Plan. Unless the Kingdom is re-established, the Grand Plan of the Father can never be realized. God gave Man dominion over the earth to rule it and take care of it, therefore the Church must make known and keep these two doctrines in remembrance to the Church.

Chapter Nine

The Kingdom Re-Established

It's Ours

Paul's student, Epaphras who had been converted in Ephesus, returned home to Colossae to proclaim the gospel and the Church is born in that city. Paul writes to the Church in Colossae and he can hardly contain himself. He has heard of their faith and the love they have toward the saints. He prays for them that they might be filled with the knowledge of His will in all wisdom and spiritual understanding in order that they may walk worthy of the Lord, fully pleasing Him, being fruitful in every good work and increasing in the knowledge of God.

What he is excited about is this; they received deliverance from the power of darkness and found a new way of living in the Kingdom of the Son of God. He is excited because now the kingdom and its culture will be established in their lives and when seen and desired by others, the Kingdom Of God will be extended.

A kingdom finds expression through its culture. Kingdom culture will find it expression in the heart of the believer, in his home, in his business, in the school, in the local church, in the local, county, state and national governments. Those living in the world will see the difference. This will awaken and excite their desire and allow the Holy Spirit opportunity to speak to their hearts.

When the Apostles went to a city, they proclaimed the Gospel of the Kingdom and then allowed the Holy Spirit to confirm the truth of their words with signs and wonders, healings and the casting out of demons.

The Kingdom of God is confirmed but it is not extended though supernatural activity. The kingdom is extended as people live-out the culture of the Kingdom on a day to day basis. This is the real proof that Jesus has re-established His Kingdom and is

73

still alive as King of the Kingdom.

"The Kingdom of God is at hand"

Jesus demonstrates throughout his earthly ministry that the Kingdom of God with all of its power had come; demons are cast out, the lame walk, the blind see and the deaf hear. Jesus sent out His 12 and His 70 and gave them the same power He possessed. This He did to show that the Kingdom was not just in Him but that His word was true when He said, *"The Kingdom of God is within you"*.

If supernatural acts were all Jesus did, He would not have re-established His Father's kingdom, because a kingdom needs citizens and territory as well as a King. He calls for people to follow Him and willing become His disciples. In His prayer to His Father He speaks of these new citizens, *"Now I am no longer in the world, but these are in the world, and I come to You. Holy Father, keep through Your name those whom You have given Me, that they may be one as We are. While I was with them in the world, I kept them in Your name. Those whom You gave Me I have kept; …John 17:11-12 (*

If He was going to influence his citizens, He needed to institute a culture that they could accept and live-out. This, Jesus did through His teaching and preaching throughout His ministry. The Sermon on the Mount is a capsule of what He taught.

Jesus was able to re-establish the Kingdom of God by satisfying the justice of God and by taking away the Keys to the Kingdom from Satan. These keys, He now gives to His Church.

When Paul writes to the Church at Corinth, he makes it clear that he does not need letters of recommendation because that were his written epistles, read by all men; clearly they were an epistle of Christ, written not by ink but by the Holy Spirit.

When writing to the Church at Thessalonica, he gives thanks to God for their work of faith, labor of love and patience of hope. He says his gospel did not come in word only but also in much power and in the Holy Spirit.

I can just see Jesus looking down at these two Churches and saying with great emotion, "NOW, That's what I'm talking about. That's Kingdom Living".

The Timing of the Kingdom

The problem for the Church today is that we are thinking like disciples instead of citizens. We are trying to be disciples by trying to be like Jesus through what we do (WWJD), instead of allowing the Holy Spirit to transform us. We are told that we are to reflect the image of Jesus; when in fact we are to be transformed into His image and unto His likeness.

The motive for our Christian work seems to be to populate heaven with God-like people instead of extending His Kingdom. We teach how to be a better you instead of teaching how to live-out Kingdom culture for the world to see. When the world sees Kingdom Culture then they will know that the King of kings and Lord of lords is alive.

You were born for a purpose just as Jesus was born for a purpose. Everyone born has been born for a purpose, whether he or she ever recognizes it or not. Jesus, in fulfilling His purpose to restore Righteousness to the earth, died and rose again. It is only by reclaiming the Father's Kingdom is Righteousness restored.

Some would say that the Kingdom of God is for the future. So is The Kingdom of God for the Future only or has Jesus come to set it up His kingdom now? Matthew tells us, *"After John was put in prison, Jesus came to Galilee, preaching the gospel of the kingdom of God, and saying, "The time is fulfilled, and the kingdom of God is at hand. Repent, and believe in the gospel."* Jesus also said, *"The Kingdom of God is within you."* He taught His disciples to pray saying, *"Our Father hallowed be thy name, thy kingdom come on earth as it is in heaven..."* Is He saying; it is now as well as future?

It is significant to know therefore, that the Kingdom is present and it is future. If we believe the Kingdom of God is only for the future, we are left to accept predeterminism as the underpinning of our Faith. With this belief, we are left with the somber thought that our Creator is Sovereign and therefore, will do whatever-whenever, as he sees fit.

Because the Kingdom of God is also now, Jesus has given to His disciples (citizens) the responsibility to continue to spread the Word that the King has come. We are to be His Ambassadors.

The Word Ambassador has no meaning if there is no

kingdom. Just because his Kingdom is not of this world, it does not mean that it has not come. It is a spiritual kingdom but it is more real than the kingdoms of this world. His kingdom will stand forever while the kingdoms of this world will pass away.

Luke, the writer of the Book of Acts, tells us that when Peter got up to address the Jews he said, *"Therefore let all the house of Israel know assuredly that God has made this Jesus, whom you crucified, both Lord and Christ."* The Jews that heard Peter understood exactly what he meant; Jesus had come to set up His kingdom, not physically but spiritual and they responded accordingly.

Satan has deceived even the "called out ones" and has caused many to think the Kingdom of God is for the future only. By his deception, he has kept the Church from advancing and if they had advanced, they would have dismantled his kingdom little by little. Because of his deception, however, there has been no opposition and Satan's kingdom has increased year after year.

We are now at a time, when all gains that have been made for the advancement of the Kingdom of God seem small in comparison. We are living at a time when many claim to be Christian, but as we look at the tree, there is no fruit. There is no faith for the miraculous, no room for the supernatural to be played out in their lives.

The Church's Future

In the study of church and secular history, we can note the changes that have taken place. Sometimes these changes were predictable and at other times, they were not. Predictable change is comfortable. It is comfortable because it comes because of cycles or foreknowledge and therefore allows for some degree of control. When we can control change, it does not control us and we just continue from the present into the future.

When change appears to be cyclical, as it has been in the past, we should stop and take note and see if it justifies making a prediction for the future. In this case, I believe it does. Struss and Howe, in their 1991 book, *Generations*, pointed out two pivotal points that represent a significant moment in the collective social life in our culture.[1] These pivotal points influence what is felt before and after them for about ten years. They have called these two points, a spiritual awakening and a secular crisis. In between these two points, they have discerned two different seasons of faith.

The last spiritual awakening took place during the 1960's and 1970's and was then followed by a season of *experiencing faith* and is related to those churches that are considered non-mainline churches (fundamental & charismatic). This was an exciting time for the Church of the Lord Jesus Christ as people from all walks of life were introduced to the Savior and were swept into the Kingdom.

However, since the mid 1990's we have entered into the second season of *doing faith* that once was only associated with the main-line churches but is now allied with the seeker friendly churches and those associated with the Social Justice movement. In each of these seasons, the churches associated with each have experienced growth and correspondingly, the other group has experienced a decline.

Since we have ended the season of *experiencing faith* and have entered into the season of *doing faith,* it suggests that we are headed for a secular crisis. We are now drawing closer and closer to this crisis every day and maybe even are experiencing its beginning.

What does that mean for the Church in general? The change that is coming certainly is not comfortable even though it is predictable. Before we address the coming change, it is healthy for us to look back and see what good and bad has occurred during the last era.

As we passed through the last spiritual awakening, we witnessed the rise of The Word of faith movement that brought back to the Church the knowledge of God's love for His people that reveal itself in supernatural ways. Millions of accounts of God's miracles of healing and deliverance have been reported throughout the whole earth. Independent/Non-denominational churches sprang up all over the world declaring the glory of God.

In the mid 1990's we began to see the other side of the coin, the emergence of the New Age movement, the anti-establishment culture, an over abundant concern for self, and a fragmentation of society where the smaller interest groups were emphasized at the expense of the national collective life. People wanted to feel good about themselves. Even in the church, we saw this happening as churches advanced the small group and cell group concept where there was less teaching and more facilitating.

Throughout the world a new awakening emerged that has taken the Church by surprise. While the Church became concerned with itself, a counterfeit gospel of the Kingdom has flooded the world and has captured the hearts of millions of young people. Some of the largest churches in America have accepted this gospel and even the White House has a new spiritual advisor that is the spokesperson for this false gospel.

In the Church, as in society, it has become nearly impossible to build a sense of *community* and agree on anything of real substance. In our society, we see the lines being drawn in the sand for just about every area of moral concern. As each side takes their positions and as each feels the strain, one wonders how soon before we will experience a national and spiritual disaster of great consequence.

What is it that now is shaping our world and therefore will shape our future? What is it that will lead up to the Big Crisis we are all dreading? We are fast becoming a global village and with it a loss of national culture. Nationalism is no longer a viable force in our global economy. Although there are a few holdouts like North Korea and Iran, the majority of the world's governments are being drawn together into bigger alliances; i.e. the United Nations. There may be a recurrence of a few border conflicts, however, the world as a whole will bring political and financial pressure and possible military force to stop the violence for the "good" of the whole.

The Church is already affected to a BIG degree. It is no longer business as usual as in the past twenty years. When there is a shift in seasons as from the "experiencing faith" to the "doing faith", there is also see a shift in values and emphasis. Whereas people were looking for spiritual experiences in the *experiencing faith* season, we see people looking now for institutions of worship that offers an expression of *doing faith* through social justice.

What is it that we can expect to see in the coming days ahead? It may be that there will be less concern with the development of one's spiritual growth. It will be a time when people will want to do faith or be involved with social or government run programs. It will be a time of embracing the familiar and be less associated with experimentation. In other words, there will be less emphasis on developing a relationship with God through the Holy Spirit and more on religion.

There will be a religious spirit that rears its ugly head within the Church. There will a form of Godliness but the people will deny the power of the Holy Spirit. This religious spirit will stand in the way of God's work. This religious spirit will cause the church leaders to talk but never say, "Thus says the Lord". It will tell the voice of the righteous to SHUT UP. It will cause the people to be lukewarm, judgmental, legalistic and critical.

It will be a time for the Great Society to rear its head. We may finally begin to see, that which we feared: the government taking over more and more control of our lives. We have already witnessed the struggle for the church to bar same sex marriages. We will see more and more of the values that we (the Church) hold dear begin to be washed away in the tide of floodwaters that are fast approaching our shores.

What is our Hope?

KINGDOM CONNECTIONS believes that our hope in bringing back righteousness to the earth depends on the Church preaching the Gospel of the Kingdom of God. This preaching must then be confirmed by the demonstration of power. There must also be a determined effort on the part of Church leaders to teach and promote the culture of the Kingdom.

The Church must not look to the past for answers but turn to the King. He has sent His Spirit into the world that He might lead and guide us. We must wait on Him and not panic but realize that the Kingdom is within us. We can go forth and bring God's Kingdom into this world along with the accompanying freedom and peace that only Jesus can give. The people of the world will

79

be drawn to us as we are transformed into His image and empowered by His Spirit. They are looking for a kingdom that presents a culture that will satisfy the longing of their soul.

Here is our problem! The disciples of Jesus Christ are waiting for the next Moses, Joshua, David, or Paul to step forward and declare, "Here is the vision that God has shared with me, come and join me". However, what is needed is a clear vision of the Kingdom by Church leaders that is then proclaimed loud and clear to body of Christ.

The Church over the last forty years has seen its acceptance increase in western culture and has grown in numbers. Because of that, pastors are reluctant to make way for change, even when that change is God directed. The material and psychological benefits that come as the Church increases in size and wealth are hard for some to give up, no matter how awesome the vision. It will take a change in our worldview to move us from our present position.

The cost of pursuing a God-given Vision is more than just surrendering to change. It demands that we give it our all, even at great sacrifice. A God-given vision is always beyond our reach. Its fulfillment can never be realized by human efforts alone; God must be involved. Moreover, when God is involved that means He is to get all the glory. Dying to self and allowing the Holy Spirit to give us a humble and meek spirit must become a priority. Our dependence must be on God's ability alone no matter how intelligent, capable or learned we are.

Accepting a God given vision is not the same as receiving a dream. Dreams given by God are sometimes foretelling of future events and at other times, they are directions to be followed. In either case, they are more or less a one-time event. A God given Vision on the other hand requires hard work, perseverance and stepping out of our comfort zone.

It sometimes means going it alone until you find others that will buy into your vision. A vision that is not mainstream and runs counter to what is generally accepted will face an uphill battle to be embraced. A God given vision pushes people into the unknown and forces them to take great risks. Those that embrace such a vision can expect to be treated the same as the Apostle Paul.

Paul, Peter, Stephen and all the other Apostles and early disciples received Jesus' vision. He said, *"Go into all the world and preach the Gospel"*. They faced opposition from their fellow Jews and from the Roman government as well. Thousands of regular every day people were crucified because they would not stop until the Vision was complete. The completion of the Vision was more important than their very lives. Listen to the Voice of Martyrs and you will hear stories of people around the world that have received this same Vision and they too are putting their lives on the line for its completion.

Where do we stand with the proclamation of the, "Gospel of the Kingdom of God"? Are we holding on to the Gospel of Jesus? The good news: that Jesus came to earth to save sinners. All you need to do is just accept him as your savior and you will be saved. When you die, you will go to heaven and live with Jesus forever.

If you accept the above, you'll not be ridiculed, be laughed at or looked upon as a heretic. However, if you catch the vision of what Jesus said and the promise of God's Grand Plan, then watch out. You will be persecuted but you will find the comfort of the Holy Spirit, you will find the strength to go on, you will find an adventure of a lifetime as you walk side by side with the King. You will be empowered by the Holy Spirit and signs and wonders will follow your spreading the Gospel of the Kingdom.

---

[1] Strauss and Howe, *Generations*

Chapter Ten

Our Journey

Getting on the Right Path

Every one of us lives, moves and plans within a certain framework of reference (a set of ideas from which we interpreted or assigned meaning to other ideas). We have considered the Topic of *Worldviews* in Chapters 1 and 2. Our worldview, in effect will become our frame of reference. We must appreciate the fact that each person has a view of the world, of life, and of eternity that is entirely their own; made up of their life experiences, including the learning that they have had. We can safely say the higher they have climbed the learning ladder, in experience and in education, the broader their perspective.

It should be of no surprise then when Jesus encourages us to come up higher, not only to learn from Him but also to see what He sees. This is important because:

- For some, their primary interest is being saved and going to heaven. This allows them to live as they like, even if it is within certain limits.

- For some, their primary interest is the establishment of God's Law and therefore become very legalistic in their approach to life.

- Others look to their new found faith in God as a way to a better life. They see their Faith as the way to prosperity, health and all other benefits that are part of their new way of life.

- Then there are those that live only to please the Father. This is where we come to our frame of reference – It is here we begin with the Father's heart even before the foundation of the world. It begins with the eternal Father and ends with a vast family of which we are a part.

"Therefore, my beloved brethren, be steadfast, immovable, always abounding in the work of the Lord, knowing that your labor is not in vain in the Lord". 1 Cor 15:58

This statement by Paul sums up his life. He is not ashamed of the Gospel and this is the work that he dedicated his life to. *When we come to understand what God's Grand Plan really is, then,* like Paul, this truth will set us free from doing anything less in importance.

Purpose and Grace

God has called us to His own purpose. Just because Adam sinned and God had to extend His mercy and grace does not mean that God forgot about or overlooked His original purpose. Our journey, to reach our destination and fulfill our purpose, is necessary in order for God to workout our perfection. It is not just a journey but a time of getting intimate with God and being prepared to fulfill His Grand Plan that He has for each of us.

Here is the problem: Most Christians are not concerned with, nor do they even know about God's purpose. They have concerned themselves only with God's grace. Because they see what God has done only as it relates to and benefits them; they do not even consider the disappointment in the Father's heart when Man lost his ability to fulfill his purpose.

Consider the following diagram as you reflect on God's original purpose. From D to Z there are steps that most Christians do not think about as they live their life out here on earth.

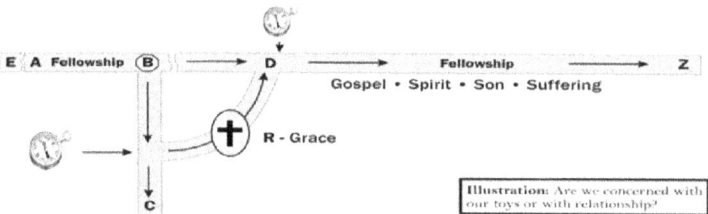

E A Fellowship (B) ——————→ D ——————→ Fellowship ——————→ Z
Gospel • Spirit • Son • Suffering

R - Grace

Illustration: Are we concerned with our toys or with relationship?

E –Eternity Past - The Correct Starting Point is The Father's Heart. All understanding of Man begins from the outpouring of the heart of the Creator, the heart of God the Father.

Our Journey

A – Creation – God made Man in His image and after His likeness. All things are created in order that man might fulfill God's Grand Plan.

B – Rebellion – When man is deceived, rebellion against his Creator is formed in his heart. This rebellion results in broken fellowship between man and his Creator. God is forced to send (drive) man out of His presence.

C – Captivity – Man, when left to his own devices, sinks further and further into captivity. His only hope is the mercy of God that reveals itself in a message of deliverance. The message when received, believed and acted upon is what brings his deliverance.

R – Redemption is the time of God's grace. By His grace, God makes it possible for mankind to be reconciled unto Him. God the Father restores us to a "child" relationship when we respond to His mercy by godly sorrow and a change in our heart from rebellion to obedience.

D – Justification – Our new position before God. We stand before God, with no condemnation and are able to move forward in fellowship and purpose with Him.

Z – The realization of God's Grand Plan for mankind – God's Grand Plan is for His children to mature and be transformed into the image and likeness of His Son, Jesus and then to rule and reign in righteousness with Him in His Kingdom.

The compass represents a "defining moment" when we make a decision that will affect us the rest of our lives. Note: The distance from B to C is best realized by viewing it as levels of Depravity. Some see their sin and need for reconciliation at an early level. Others travel down the road of depravity, becoming the outcasts of society, before coming to repentance and faith in Christ (Nicky Cruz of "*The Cross and the Switchblade*").

There are other "defining moments" that allow us to go deeper into the love of God. However, we must realize that each one is not the goal or the end in itself. *Conviction* of sin is not our desired result nor is the *Forgiveness* that follows. We might think that the *Reconciliation*, which comes next, is what God desires for us, but it is not. It is not even the *Relationship* that evolves. What

God wants is for us to enter into an intense, intimate *Fellowship* with Him.

Is our goal D or is the goal Z? If our goal is D then we will rally around the cross and never move on toward the Grand Plan that God has for us.

However, if our goal is Z we must be involved in two tasks. First, we must take our renewed relationship (redemption) through four levels of Fellowship. Second, we must grasp and take hold of our understanding regarding our reinstated position (justification). We will discuss the second in Chapter 12.

God's desire is for us to participate in 'fellowship'. Our English word, 'fellowship' is the translation of the Greek word, "*koinonia.*" In New Testament times this word was used to describe a joint-partnership in a business venture in which all parties actively participate to ensure the success of the business.[1]

In addition to being translated as fellowship it is also translated by the words, "contribution," "sharing," and "participation." A close study of the usage of this word shows that action is always included in its meaning. Fellowship is not just being together, it is doing together! It is our partnership with Christ in fulfilling God's will.

Fellowship is an inner unity expressed outwardly in action. It is not just being together but doing together. It is not just doing anything together but it is working together to accomplish God's will.

If we are going to continue on this journey, we must not only understand why this word was used but also understand the levels of and the depth of this 'Fellowship' that God calls us.[2]

The journey continues as we participate in the (a) Fellowship of His Gospel. We move along as we engage in the (b) Fellowship of His Spirit. As we offer ourselves as a living sacrifice, we are growing in the (c) Fellowship of His Son. The real test of our love is when we enter into the (d) Fellowship of His Sufferings.

God's has a Purpose for Man. To understand the importance of this call into fellowship we must understand God's purpose for Man. The Bible testifies to God's thoughts regarding this:

- *"Let us make man in our image and after our likeness and let them have dominion"* (Gen. 1:26-28)

- *"Be ye therefore perfect, even as your father in heaven is perfect"* (Matt. 5:48)

- *"This also we wish, even your perfection"* (2 Cor. 13:9)

- *"I travail in birth until Christ be formed in you"* (Gal. 4:9)

- *"Until we all come...unto a perfect man* (Eph. 4:13)

- *"That the man of God be perfect"* (2 Tim. 3:17)

- *"Hath called us unto glory and virtue"* (2 Pet. 1:3)

This purpose has never changed. Jesus is the first born of many sons. Hebrews 2:10 says, *"For it was fitting for Him, for whom are all things and by whom are all things, in bringing many sons to glory, to make the captain of their salvation perfect through sufferings."*

In addition, in Hebrews 1:8-9, *"But to the Son He says: "Your throne, O God, is forever and ever; a scepter of righteousness is the scepter of your kingdom. You have loved righteousness and hated lawlessness; Therefore God, Your God, has anointed You with the oil of gladness more than your companions."*

Levels of Fellowship

(a) Fellowship in the Gospel - Philippians 1:3-6

I thank my God upon every remembrance of you, always in every prayer of mine making request for you all with joy, for your fellowship in the gospel from the first day until now, being confident of this very thing, that He who has begun a good work in you will complete it until the day of Jesus Christ;

All Christians enjoy this common experience. It can be a very shallow experience or one of some substance. The more we have knowledge of His will, stand in agreement with His plan, grow in our affection toward Him, enjoy His presence, conform to His image, and participate in His joy the more we deepen our Fellowship of the Gospel. This is a result of spending time reading the Word and in prayer.

When you join with others in this Fellowship of the Gospel, you are in effect joining a TEAM and become a member of its culture. When you join or fellowship at a particular church; you are joining their team. Even if there are only two of you, you are a team. The Apostle Paul continually admonished the Church to have the same mind; showing the world, that those that embrace the gospel can work in unity, they can love the unlovable, and they can forgive as they are forgiven.

Disciples are not just followers; they are messengers of the gospel. We are called out from the world to be Ambassadors of the Kingdom. The early disciples knew they were reconciled to Christ and that God was making his appeal to the world through them. There was a love that was placed within them that took a hold of their heart; they were convinced that Jesus died for all, was raised from the dead that they might no longer live for themselves but for Him.

Jesus' plan was simple. He brought together a team of twelve men who were dedicated to Him and His message. For three years He lived with, cared for, taught, corrected, trusted, forgave, and loved them. He prepared them for service and He expected them to go forth and do the same for others as He had done for them.

We are now 21st Century Disciples of Christ therefore; we hold dear, not just the teachings of Jesus, but also the person of Jesus himself. The Gospel of the Kingdom is revolutionary. It changes the heart. The Gospel, powered by His Spirit, is a gospel of love that transforms every one of us from the inside out.

No other gospel offers such promise and hope to humanity. It offers to bring man out darkness into the light. It offers peace to the troubled. It offers freedom to those that are bound. It offers forgiveness of sin, mercy, grace, health, prosperity and righteousness. It offers a future with life everlasting instead of torment and pain. When the truth of this gospel consumes us, as it did Jesus and the early Church, we will turn our world upside down.

When you are on a team, you need to have the same purpose, the same vision, the same attitude and the same level of faith or at least open to grow in your faith. You need to come under the same governmental authority or you will be divided. When you are on a team, everyone participates and the greater opportunity for success.

The question is: Is the team you're on even in the game? Is the church you are attending even out there sharing the Gospel?

(b) Fellowship of the Spirit - Philippians 2:1-3

"Therefore if there is any consolation in Christ, if any comfort of love, if any fellowship of the Spirit, if any affection and mercy, fulfill my joy by being like-minded, having the same love, being of one accord, of one mind."

God calls us to be led by the Spirit of God in order that we can live a righteous life without condemnation. We are to walk after the Spirit and not after the flesh. This relationship with the Holy Spirit is an intense and personal relationship. When we are involved in sin, the Holy Spirit is grieved and He will quickly depart. He is unable to move in our lives when we do not allow him access to our spirit. He comes to empower us, yet He will back off when we decide to do our own thing, ignore him, or do it our own way.

To walk in fellowship of the Spirit requires a willingness to go in the same direction as the Holy Spirit. It means that we must walk together with the same conviction of purpose, hand in hand and shoulder to shoulder.

God the Father gave Jesus the responsibility to re-claim the Kingdom; this He did by the power of the Holy Spirit. Now it is time for His disciples to extend the Kingdom by the same power of the Holy Spirit. Just as Jesus relied on the Holy Spirit to accomplish His task, we must do the same to accomplish ours.

The power of the Holy Spirit is not separate from the person of the Holy Spirit. Without his presence, there is no power. Without fellowship with the Holy Spirit, our work for the Lord is our work and not His. The early disciples recognized this and joined themselves together, prayed together, worshiped together and experienced together the infilling of the Holy Spirit. They held all things in common and the Holy Spirit was pleased. He manifested His presence and the gifts of the Spirit were available to carry on the Work assigned.

Jesus said, *"I still have many things to say to you, but you cannot bear them now. However, when He, the Spirit of truth, has come, He will guide you into all truth; for He will not speak on His own authority, but whatever He hears He will speak; and He will tell you things to come. He will glorify Me, for He will take of what is Mine and declare it to you. All things that the Father has are Mine. Therefore, I said that He will take of Mine and declare it to you."* (John 16:12-15).

We continue to emphasis, that we must develop our relationship with the Holy Spirit. If we only talk about Jesus and only mention the Father when we pray, we will soon become legalistic. Furthermore, we will begin to "reason out" Scripture instead of receiving revelation from the one who has been given the responsibility to be the administrator of the Church.

Since the Holy Spirit is a spirit, it is only through our spirit that we can sense his presence. We, therefore, must develop our sensitivity to the Holy Spirit.

(c) Fellowship of the Son - 1 Corinthians 1:4-9

"I thank my God always concerning you for the grace of God which was given to you by Christ Jesus, that you were enriched in everything by Him in all utterance and all knowledge, even as the testimony of Christ was confirmed in you, so that you come short in no gift, eagerly waiting for the revelation of our Lord Jesus Christ, who will also confirm you to the end, that you may be blameless in the day of our Lord Jesus Christ. God is faithful, by whom you were called into the fellowship of His Son, Jesus Christ our Lord."

As the Holy Spirit lives to make Christ more real, we realize that we are called to go still further and deeper into Fellowship. We are exhorted to offer our total self as a living sacrifice, to have the mind of Christ, to abide in Christ, to listen to and to obey Christ. We are called to an intimacy closer than that of a husband and wife. There are no secrets, there is no doubt, there is no fear, and there is no holding back of love and sacrifice for the other. There is nothing not shared.

To have fellowship with the Son, we must align our life to having the same purpose in life as Him. We must walk in the light as He is in the light and be willing to take up our cross (the assignment that God has given to us). This fellowship with the

Son involves more than our heart, it involves our feet, hands and mouth. It involves our "doing". There is no fellowship with the Son without our participating in the same work of extending His Kingdom.

More about our Fellowship with the Son follows in Chapter Eleven when we discuss "The Son of Man" and the "Internal Cross".

(d) Fellowship of His sufferings – Philippians 3:7-11

"But what things were gain to me, these I have counted loss for Christ. Yet indeed I also count all things loss for the excellence of the knowledge of Christ Jesus my Lord, for whom I have suffered the loss of all things, and count them as rubbish, that I may gain Christ and be found in Him, not having my own righteousness, which is from the law, but that which is through faith in Christ, the righteousness which is from God by faith; that I may know Him and the power of His resurrection, and the fellowship of His sufferings, being conformed to His death, if, by any means, I may attain to the resurrection from the dead."

As we present ourselves to grow in greater fellowship with our Lord, we find that it is no longer us that live, but Christ who lives in us. We find that we now consider ourselves crucified with Christ, dead to sin and alive unto God. We identify with His purposes not ours.

It is as we respond to this call to Fellowship in His Sufferings that we are prepared to enter into fruitful ministry. We must maintain our focus on His Purpose and embrace God's Grand Plan, or we will not continue on this pathway to the throne – we will take the road less traveled. See 2 Cor. 11:23-30; Phil 1:20; 2 Cor. 4: 7-11; 2 Cor. 1:1-7.

If we look around the Church today, it soon becomes obvious that men occupy themselves with only various parts of truth. It also becomes evident, that the depths of the truths we accept and our willingness to stand against the opposing arguments will reveal the "level of our fellowship."

There is no book that has stirred my heart in recent years than, *Tortured for Christ* by Richard Wurmbrand, founder of The Voice of the Martyrs. From the writings in this small volume, I began to see the true meaning of the Fellowship of His

Sufferings. Suffering for righteousness sake involves more than the brutality of physical or mental cruelty.

The ungodly lash out to those that bring light into darkness. They do not want their evil deeds to be exposed. They want to protect their self-righteous image and their place in society; whether that society is family, work or community. They want to quiet the voices of those that speak up for righteousness, just as the Jewish people killed the prophets in the Old Testament. They will use ridicule, belittlement and lies to discredit the messenger of the very message that can bring them the freedom and peace that they seek.

The ungodly will use fear to persuade the righteous to back off from their rigid stand against them. They threaten to steal, kill, not only the body, but all our dreams and visions, and destroy or eradicate any sense of purpose that keeps us moving forward. They wish to crush our spirit.

Listen to Paul's comments to the Church at Corinth after his ordeals; 2 Corinthians 4. *"But we have this treasure in earthen vessels, that the excellence of the power may be of God and not of us. We are hard-pressed on every side, yet not crushed; we are perplexed, but not in despair; persecuted, but not forsaken; struck down, but not destroyed — always carrying about in the body the dying of the Lord Jesus, that the life of Jesus also may be manifested in our body. For we who live are always delivered to death for Jesus' sake, that the life of Jesus also may be manifested in our mortal flesh."*

Satan hates God's servants. When we attack his kingdom, he takes notice and assigns higher-level powers to go on the defensive. He may use family members, friends, fellow church members and even your community to stop your attack.

The question: How long will you and I continue in this fellowship of suffering as we travel toward the throne? When we have deeply entered into this fellowship with our God we find that we are participating fully with Him in His Grand Plan.

---

[1] NKJV-Annotations, Philippians 1:5 page 1997
[2] DeVern F. Fromke, *The Ultimate Intention*

Chapter Eleven

Servant and King

The Son of Man

The Bible uses the term Son of Man 82 times in the New Testament. All, but two, are from the lips of Jesus himself. We have to wonder, why did Jesus make known this self-chosen title for Himself?

The biggest obstacle that Jesus faced was that of identity. He needed to communicate to the people of the day exactly who he was. He was not just a teacher, prophet or a priest. He was a king and not just any king but the promised messiah-the King of Glory. He needed a title that would identify himself and his mission. He needed a title that the people could recognize but the title itself could be used it in such a way that it would shock them into listening.

The title comes from Daniel 7:13-14. *"I was watching in the night visions, And behold, one like the Son of Man, Coming with the clouds of heaven! He came to the Ancient of Days, and they brought Him near before Him. Then to Him was given dominion, glory, and a kingdom that all peoples, nations, and languages should serve Him. His dominion is an everlasting dominion, which shall not pass away,"*

Daniel had a vision of four empires that were so cruel that they were called beasts. However, Daniel, in his vision, was revealing that the time of their power had ended and that a new empire was coming. In Dan 7:18, he writes, *"But the saints of the Most High shall receive the kingdom, and possess the kingdom forever, even forever and ever."* The King that was to come was "The Messiah".

Because of this vision, the Nation of Israel had the expectation, that when they hear that the Son of Man has come they could expect the return of their glorious empire as under King David. This new victorious King would be the long awaited Messiah.

In Mark 2:5-12 we read of the story of the paralyzed man lowered through the roof so that Jesus could heal him. *"When Jesus saw their faith, He said to the paralytic, 'Son, your sins are forgiven you.' And some of the scribes were sitting there and reasoning in their hearts, 'Why does this Man speak blasphemies like this? Who can forgive sins but God alone?'"*

But immediately, when Jesus perceived in His spirit that they reasoned thus within themselves, He said to them, "Why do you reason about these things in your hearts? Which is easier, to say to the paralytic, 'Your sins are forgiven you,' or to say, 'Arise, take up your bed and walk'?

But that you may know that the SON OF MAN *has power on earth to forgive sins"* — *He said to the paralytic, "I say to you, arise, take up your bed, and go to your house." Immediately he arose, took up the bed, and went out in the presence of them all, so that all were amazed and glorified God, saying, "We never saw anything like this!"*

Jesus proclaimed that He was God but said more by what He called Himself, The Son of Man. Jesus, by identifying himself as the Son of Man, He was proclaiming to be the Messiah and therefore, ushering in the Kingdom that would have dominion forever and forever.

However, the Nation of Israel, having been subjected to humiliation and dishonor, was not looking for a gentle and humane Messiah. They could not imagine a Messiah, such as the man named Jesus, who could lead them to greatness and power.

How they got to this point is possibly based on the Inter-testament book of Enoch. In this book, the Son of Man is always a divine figure waiting in the heavenly places to be unleashed in vengeance and in judgment upon the world. He reigns in triumph and then shares that triumph with the faithful.

Also in Psalm 2:7, a psalm long regarded as a Messianic Psalm, it speaks of the Son begotten of God and pictures His triumph and the judgment executed upon His enemies. *"I will declare the decree: the Lord hath said unto me, Thou art my Son; this day have I begotten thee. Ask of me, and I shall give thee the heathen for thine inheritance, and the uttermost parts of the earth for thy possession. Thou shalt break them with a rod of iron; thou shalt dash them in pieces like a potter's vessel"*

93

Nevertheless, the following two Scriptures reveal yet another picture of the Messiah. They bring together the idea of the suffering servant and the triumphant Messiah in Jesus.

In Isaiah 42:1, the writer begins to draw his picture of God's servant but does not complete it until he puts the finishing strokes to the canvas in Isaiah 53.

When Jesus speaks of himself as the Son of Man, we see him as someone who has nowhere to lay his head, is persecuted and as one who has come to seek and save the lost. He identifies himself as one coming, not to be served but to serve and to give his life as a ransom for many; not coming to destroy men's lives but to save them.

The disciples were at first confused and not ready to accept this new picture of their Messiah. Even though Jesus spoke often of his death and the resurrection, they still could not see the complete picture because of what was already painted in their mind; that of a conquering king who would destroy their enemies and pronounce judgment upon them.

The reason for the above goes back to what we discussed regarding the Jellybeans. The human mind will shut off anything that it does not expect to see, accept or understand. The disciples connected the Son of Man with majesty, power and glory, not with the idea of suffering, humiliation and death.

It was the resurrection that made the difference in the thinking of the disciples. If the story ended with His suffering and death, it would have been impossible for the early Church to see Jesus as the fulfillment of the Son of Man as depicted by Isaiah. The resurrection however, brought the suffering, the triumph, and the glory together to complete the picture.

Be of the Same Mind

If we are to delight in the fellowship of the Son, and therefore realize God's Grand Plan of reigning with Him, we must see ourselves as servants; while at the same time know that we are royalty. This is the point of seeing Jesus as the Son of Man.

This is not an easy task. We are to humble ourselves to be servants and at the same time be meek that we might exercise our position as Royalty.

God was not satisfied with just giving man a natural family and a material dwelling. God did not just crate man who was then to be on his own. But in His wisdom, He brought man into His house, not as a servant but as a son.

- *For as many as are led by the Spirit of God, these are sons of God. For, you did not receive the spirit of bondage again to fear, but you received the Spirit of adoption by whom we cry out, "Abba, Father." The Spirit Himself bears witness with our spirit that we are children of God, and if children, then heirs — heirs of God and joint heirs with Christ, if indeed we suffer with Him, that we may also be glorified together.* (Rom. 8:15-17, emphasis added)

- *For it was fitting for Him, for whom are all things and by whom are all things, in bringing many sons to glory, to make the captain of their salvation perfect through sufferings. For both He who sanctifies and those who are being sanctified are all of one, for which reason He is not ashamed to call them brethren, saying: "I will declare Your name to My brethren; In the midst of the assembly I will sing praise to You."* (Heb 2:10-12, emphasis added)

God the Father makes all His plans with the Son in mind. His goal is that in the coming ages, Jesus might have a glorious body in which to express His very life. This body is a family of brothers and sisters whom He might have fellowship and would share His reign.

2 Tim 2:11-12

This is a faithful saying: For if we died with Him,
We shall also live with Him. If we endure,
We shall also reign with Him.

Rev 20:6

Blessed and holy is he who has part in the first resurrection. Over such the second death has no power, but they shall be priests of God and of Christ, and shall reign with Him a thousand years.

Rev 3:21

*To him who overcomes I will grant to sit with Me on My throne, as I
also overcame and sat down with My Father on His throne.*

The Internal Cross-God's Guiding Principle

In order for us to understand the Divine Principle that guides
all of God's actions, we need to comprehend the relationship that
exists in the Godhead, between the Father, Son and Holy Spirit.
The basis of our Christian belief is that we acknowledge that
there is one God existing as three eternal and co-equal Beings,
the same in substance (essence) but distinct in subsistence (life).

Each has a different role to execute in this relationship. The
Father is the authority while the Son fulfills the will of the
Father. The Spirit speaks not of Himself but dedicates His
activities to revealing the Son and fulfilling the desires of the
Father and the Son.

The Father's intent is to exalt His Son who is under His
authority and the Son serves that authority so that his purposes
can be carried out. This is a relationship where there is no
conflict and where there is perfect unity. The one in authority
uses His authority benevolently for the good of those under Him
and the one under Him responds with respect and with a
servant's heart.

It is God's desire that we experience the same fellowship,
love, peace, joy and unity of purpose that exists in the Godhead.
In other words, our relationships here on earth should be such
that, no one lives for themselves but for each other.

Point to Embrace: What the Father, Son and Holy Spirit are
revealing to the Church today is that there was not only an
external cross (Calvary) **but also there is an "internal" Cross.**

The Fruit of the Spirit: love, joy, peace, longsuffering,
gentleness, goodness, faith, meekness, temperance, is a result of
the Holy Spirit flowing through us. It is also the result of the
internal cross in us. You cannot separate the manifestation of
God's presence from the person of God. You cannot separate the

cross principal from God and you cannot separate the "internal cross" from the Christian. "Internal" expresses the POWER that is in the word itself.

As the gold thread in the Priest's garment is interwoven into the fabric, so the cross must be interwoven into the fabric of our lives. The gold is separate from the other threads but it is such an integrated part of the design that it cannot be removed without destroying the cloth and therefore the garment.

In order for God to reclaim His Kingdom, man must be set free from the bondage to sin and be declared justified. To accomplish this, God has revealed the external Cross of Christ that we might understand the character of His love.

The real problem for man is this: man sees the cross only as it relates to him. He does not see how it relates to God and to the realizing of His Grand Plan.[1]

Man was created to be a body for the Son that He might express Himself in the Earth and be a joint heir with Him. Salvation from Hell is not the main reason for the Son's coming to earth but a necessary reclaiming action (an action to fix a problem).

In the garden, Adam missed seeing the "Internal" Cross of the Father. It was the desire of the Father that this "Internal" Cross be in His children as it is in Him and in His only begotten Son. It was to be their manner and purpose in life, a guiding principle. You are invited to embrace the Cross Principle as a manner of life. It cannot be thrust upon you. It is not just to be chosen once – at the time of salvation - but must become the principle that guides all your actions.

If we are going to take this journey toward fulfilling God's Grand Plan, we must understand and embrace the following CENTRAL TRUTH – The Cross is an inherent part of the character of God as it is demonstrated by the Son and revealed by the Holy Spirit. This same principle must also be the guiding rule in our life.

---

[1] DeVern Fromke, *The Ultimate Intention*

Chapter Twelve

"What is that in your Hand?"

Life subject to a New Ruler

In Chapter Ten, we considered that our renewed relationship (redemption) takes us down the pathway through four levels of Fellowship. Now we will consider another aspect of our journey as we come to understand our reinstated position (justification).

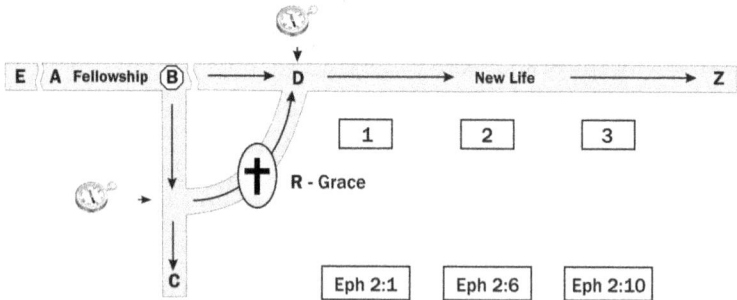

As we progress down the Pathway to the Throne, Paul emphasizes that there are three areas of New Life training that we must go through. 1. The New Life we are living has **Resurrection Power**; for we are made alive with Christ, 2. The New Life we are living has **Royal Power**; for we are seated with Christ in the heavenly places, 3. The New Life we are now living has **Realizing Power**; for the life of God is being manifested through us to be a blessing to others.

Resurrection Power

The Cross brings death to the "old-self" life but without Resurrection Power to raise us from death, we would not be able to live in newness of life. We would be free from the penalty of sin but not able to live with power over sin. Resurrection Power is the Power for a New Life.

In Chapter 1 we studied the importance of the mind. When we begin to think differently, we begin to act differently. Paul tells us to offer our total being as a sacrifice to God. He then tells us we need to think differently when he says, *"be not conformed to this world but be transformed by the renewing of your mind"*. This is a must for us because until we were "born again", we were slaves to the desires of the flesh and subject to the prince of the power of the air. These habits of the flesh now have to be overcome.

Just as the Father did not leave Jesus to suffer corruption in death, so He does not leave us to suffer without power to live a new life without righteousness. He has made us alive in Christ because it is our faith and identification with Him that allows us to walk in this newness of life. Paul writes to the Church in Galatia, that he is no longer finding righteousness by trying to adhere to the Law but he is in fact dead to the Law. He has had a transformation in his mind and spirit by faith; he has died with Christ and the resurrected Christ now lives in him. The life he is now living he lives by faith in the Son of God who loves him.

This Resurrection Power that we now possess, allows us to consider ourselves dead to sin and alive unto God. Sin no longer reigns in our body because we have power; a power greater than sin. Sin will have no more dominion over us because we are not under the law but under grace.

The Apostle Paul writes, *"And I pray your whole spirit and soul and body be preserved blameless unto the coming of our Lord Jesus Christ."* (1 Thess. 5:23). He writes this because he knows that the Lord is coming back for a glorious Church without spot or wrinkle, a victorious Church full of power.

If we are not living in this Resurrection Power, then our travel down the pathway to the throne will be filled with disillusionment, despair, heartache and hopelessness. You will be like Lot's wife who turned around to look back at that which had been left behind and was turned into a pillar of salt or the farmer Jesus describes when He said, *"No one, having put his hand to the plow, and looking back, is fit for the kingdom of God."* (Luke 9:62).

Royal Power

Resurrection Power by itself would have been enough to shout about but God has even better things in store for His redeemed. The Father does not want to wait until His wrath is fully unleashed against the devil and he is banished to the Lake Fire forever before He exercises dominion over His earth.

From the beginning, He has decreed that Man would have dominion over the earth. He is not going to usurp man's authority and take control himself. He already had devised a plan that would allow man to start having dominion even before Christ returns as King of kings and Lord of lords.

This heavenly sphere is not just a place out there in the universe. The heaven that Paul is referring to is the highest place. It is the seat of His government. It is the place of much activity. Angels are being dispatched throughout the whole earth as ministering spirit to the saints. There are voices that sound like thunder when the Father is speaking.

King Jesus is ruling in the lives of the Redeemed by the power of the Holy Spirit. Angels are opening the vaults of heaven as the saints are using the Keys of the Kingdom to unlock the blessings of heaven. Because of our position with Christ in the heavenlies, Believers are using His name to heal the sick and to cast out demons, setting the captives FREE.

Royalty does not need to be in the place of government to exercise its rule. Because of our identity with Christ, we can rule here on Earth as his representatives and as part of the royal family. By virtue of our position (having been justified and sitting, by identification, with Christ in the Heavenlies), we have been given the RIGHT to rule and take dominion; not because of our self-righteousness but because of Christ's.

Christ has ALL authority and He has given to us, His royal brethren, more than the right to use this authority, but has commissioned us to go forth and continue the works of God until all nations are under His feet.

Realizing Power

We are mindful always of what God has done for us. We are mindful that we are the bride of Christ and one day we will be summoned to the marriage feast of the Lamb. We are mindful that we will someday stand before the judgment seat of Christ. We are mindful that our works will be judged worthy, as by fire and the clothing we will wear, as a wedding garment will be the undergarment of the righteousness of Christ and the outer garment of the good works that survived the fire.

Realizing power is a power that we put to use each and every day to reckon ourselves dead to sin and alive unto God. It is a power within that causes us to achieve our goal of living for Christ. It is a power that heals the sick, cast out demons, raises the dead, performs miracles and performs signs and wonders. It feeds the hungry, gives drink to the thirsty, clothes the naked and visits those in prison.

As we embrace each of the above components of our New Life, we are progressing toward becoming an *Overcomer*. As we become an Overcomer, we will show power over sin and over our enemy in our life. As an Overcomer, we will take authority over our enemy and take back what he has stolen. As an Overcomer, we will show forth His glory in all that we do as we live unto God.

Leadership Effectiveness Training

In the late 80's and early 90's I conducted management seminars for small businesses and leadership Seminars for Pastors. In these seminars, I taught that there are three phases of growth that each must go through in order to achieve success. Growth has to occur in Character, Ability and Leadership.

Maturing: The Bible speaks of a person, having matured into adulthood, as having reached a place in their life as being responsible, trustworthy, faithful, unconditional in love and their attitude toward work and giving. It represents a life of being in oneness with God. The Father has given to the Spirit the work of maturing the new child of God and bringing about full-Sonship. The Father gives as a gift –His life, His nature, His Spirit.

Nevertheless, growth into the very character of Jesus is the product of training, overcoming, discipline, trial, hardship, and intensive spiritual qualifying. (See 2 Tim 2:15; 3:16.)

The outstanding characteristic of the modern day Church goes beyond shallowness, it borders on superficiality. Our attitude toward the Bible reveals that we have not taken it seriously. We must take it as it is, and allow it to speak to us. Reading the Bible is not enough. It takes thought and meditation or we will read into Scripture the results of our own reasoning and that will be to our own destruction. Because of our lack of accurate knowledge, we will make the wrong assumptions and then draw the wrong conclusions.

To bring about maturity in the Believer, is the job of the Church and Family working with the Holy Spirit. The Church, however, has changed from having a Fathering mentality (using the five-fold ministry gifts to mentor the saints) to a church of attendees who are spectators and consumers of a "bless me" message given by a one-man show.

The Church must decide what they are going to present to their adherents based on what God has called them to do. Maturing has to do with both relationships and doing good works. The Church must begin to mature its people in the area of citizenship and prepare them to be Overcomers.

Preparing: The Apostle John tells us that Jesus increased in wisdom and in stature. Therefore, if we desire to reign with Him we also must increase in wisdom and stature.

We are destined for the throne but we must be prepared to reign. This is our inheritance. We must go through many varied experiences in order that our lives are thoroughly brought under the control of the Holy Spirit.

These experiences are like doors that we must pass through. We must surrender to the purpose of each experience. As we pass through each door, we gain wisdom. When it is our time to reign with Christ, we will use this wisdom for His glory.

We must keep our eyes on God's Grand Plan – His Purpose. If not, our experiences will not be inter-connected and they will not lead to our destination. As a train must be on the track and all the cars must be connected, so our experiences must be related and in line with the Father's purpose.

This is so very different from the present day explanation given for Romans 8:28-29, "And *we know that all things work together for good to those who love God, to those who are the called according to His purpose.*" The Church today presents this verse as saying – Whatever comes our way it is God's will and we are to accept it. The church totally ignores the fact that we must be walking in accordance to His purpose. It is then and only then, things will work out for our good.

We may be "born again" but this alone does not qualify us to reign. To participate in all that preparation encompasses, comes only to those who live unto the Father's purpose. Paul admonishes us when he writes, *"Brethren, do not be children in understanding; however, in malice be babes, but in understanding be mature."* (1 Cor. 14:20).

Discussion: What then do we make of certain genuine experiences, such as salvation, separation, consecration, Baptism in the Holy Spirit, healing? Can these be just like a series of crises through which the Holy Spirit leads the hungry heart in its quest for truth or are they to prepare us for something we are to do?

Governing: Governing is more than leadership. Leadership is more than management. It is both of these put together plus the additional availability of both power and authority.

Wisdom is needed if one is to govern and this wisdom comes from God alone. It is not just sitting upon a throne, but executing righteousness in doing the will of the Father that speaks of our right to rule.

To qualify for the throne, it requires that we have passed the test when confronted by our enemy and are willing to face the stones and arrows of this world. It requires that we have shown the righteous exercise of authority over the domain that we have been given. It requires that we have remained obedient even in the face of suffering. Paul is a perfect example of someone who experienced the beatings and then writes from that experience when he says:

- *The Spirit Himself bears witness with our spirit that we are children of God, and if children, then heirs — heirs of God and joint heirs with Christ, if indeed we suffer with Him, that we may also be glorified together.* (Rom. 8:16-18)

- *If we endure, we shall also reign with Him.* (2 Tim 2:12)

God's first call to Man was for him to have dominion over the earth and his last call to him is to reign with Him above the highest heavens. To enter into such joint position with the Lord Jesus is almost beyond our comprehension. However, to rule in righteousness is our mandate.

The writer of Hebrews states in Chapter 1, verses 8-9, AMP, *"But as to the Son, He says to Him, Your throne, O God, is forever and ever (to the ages of the ages), and the scepter of Your kingdom is a scepter of absolute righteousness - of justice and straightforwardness. You have loved righteousness - You delighted in integrity, virtue and uprightness in purpose, thought and action - and you have hated lawlessness (injustice and iniquity)."* (Emphasis added).

A scepter is a symbolic ornamental staff held by a ruling monarch, a prominent item of royal regalia. The scepter represents authority and often represents how a monarch will rule.[2]

Our concept of governing must come from only one source, God Himself. If we do not have within us the realization that we are to one-day rule and reign with Christ, we will remain - knowing but never doing. We must be transformed to acquire a heart of a ruler. There are some in the Church that understand the concept of the kingdom, having dominion and taking authority over sin, sickness and poverty but still have never received the vision of ruling with Christ.

The Peter Principle is the principle that says, "In a hierarchy every employee tends to rise to his level of incompetence." In other words, its members are promoted so long as they work competently but then are promoted to a position they are no longer proficient and then remain there until they leave. In the Kingdom of God it is not based on our ability but on our availability. It is the Holy Spirit that empowers us to do and succeed.

Created to Rule

To satisfy His desire to share His life with another, God the Father created a visible kingdom that mirrored the invisible Kingdom of Heaven. In order to share His life, He created Man. The wonder of the creation of Man is that he can communicate with his King although He is in the spiritual realm while he is in the physical.

If God was going to create earth and establish upon it a kingdom to rule, He must either rule it himself or put someone else in charge. A king does not appoint a non-citizen or a slave to rule over his kingdom. To do so would put his kingdom at peril. A king looks for loyal, trusted, tested, honest and trustworthy men and women to put in such an important position. He confers this honor to citizens that take an "oath of allegiance".

Do you consider yourself a loyal citizen of the Kingdom or just a slave or a servant to Jesus? Do you consider yourself a citizen of the Kingdom of God, ready to fulfill your destiny and the hope of your calling each and every day?

This message of the Gospel of the Kingdom of God is the "Good News" that Jesus invites all into His Father's kingdom. In addition, upon entry He restores their citizenship rights and makes it possible for them to represent his Father's kingdom by giving to them His Spirit. This is why throughout this book we have been talking about God's Grand Plan. That plan has always been for the Father to have a family of sons like unto his only begotten Son, Jesus.

It is the Father's intent for the Son of God to have brethren in which He could express himself here on earth and for the Holy Spirit to have a temple in which to dwell and manifest the power of God. This can only be accomplished through a maturing process. It is our Father's Grand Plan that we will someday rule and reign with His only begotten Son, Jesus. The unusual aspect about all this is that all the mature citizens are sons of the Father.

Unless you know that you are a Citizen of the Kingdom of God, you will never still the storm, cast out devils, heal the sick, raise the dead, or turn water into wine.

Chapter Thirteen

A Son Placed

Adoption

There are many varied renderings of the meaning of adoption used throughout the Old Testament. Some of these are very similar to the meaning that is in use today. In the New Testament, only Paul uses this word.

We must understand that God does not "adopt" believers as children; they are "Born Again" into His family by the Holy Spirit, through faith.

"Adoption" is a term involving the dignity of the relationship of believers as sons; it is not a putting into the family by spiritual birth, but a putting into the position as sons. The term as used in a theological sense commonly denotes, "a specific act of God by which He restores penitent and believing men to their privileges as members of the divine family and makes them heirs of heaven."[1]

In the parable of the prodigal son, the wayward son returns home glad to confess that he is unworthy to be called a son. He had dismissed the desire of the Father to be of little consequence and of little value. Just as Esau had sold his birthright, the prodigal son had walked away from his inheritance. The point to be observed is; that by Redemption and Justification, the prodigal son was not only forgiven and reconciled to his merciful father; he was restored to the position of a son. This gracious act of his father enabled him to receive his inheritance. It was if he had never rebelled at all.

Adoption has the thought behind it of a "son placed". It was the practice of kings to place their sons, heirs to their throne, under the tutelage of professionals. These teachers would train them in all aspects of becoming a ruler of the kingdom. Kings gave to the tutors the responsibility of instilling into their sons, the very heart of the king. We learn from the life of Moses, that "when he was fully grown" he went out to visit his relatives. The "fully grown" suggests that when the Egyptians had completed his training, he went out to visit the Hebrews.

On a lower level; in the early sixties, I completed a two-year apprenticeship. When completed, I received a diploma, was elevated to the title of journeymen, and received a substantial raise. It was at this point that I was now accepted into an elite group of bottle makers.

Today, when a man has established himself in business and has a son, his greatest hope is that his son will follow his example and take over the business. He does not take this casually. Over the years, he has put his sweat, blood and tears in the building of his business. His desire is for his son to run his business with the same dedication, the same set of values and principles that he ascribed to and will continue to build the business so that he might pass it on to his children. This training may involve working in the business as a janitor, a stock boy, salesperson, etc, and most assuredly in today's economy, going to the university.

In the day of Apostle Paul, male children were placed in the hands of entrusted servants to train and teach them to act and think in such a way as to prepare them for the life they were to lead upon becoming of age. Today, those of wealth and position still send their daughters off to 'finishing school'.

God has given Gifts to all of his children. Do we need people working in the church parking lot? Do we need people in the choir? Yes. Do we need people teaching the young children and in nursery? Yes. Do we need people working in the offices and others maintaining our campuses? Yes. All these endeavors are necessary but not at the expense of the most needed; which is, that these same people are to be using the Gifts of the Spirit in accomplishing their task. How can we say that the Holy Spirit has "Free reign" in our services when man is in control and there is little or no evidence of His presence?

How are we going to rule and reign with Christ when we are not given, either the opportunity for a mentor to show us how to be led by the Spirit or the training to operate in the gifts of the Spirit?

It is time that the Church takes seriously the orders that it has received from the Lord of the Church to prepare His bride for His return. We would think it was a dereliction of duty if a college did not prepare its students to enter the work force with the appropriate training or our armed forces to send troops into battle without the right training. Why then do we not think it is a dereliction of duty for the Church to send it members out unprepared to fight against it enemies, let alone unprepared to rule and reign with Christ?

Can You Imagine

Prince William, when he was born, was heir apparent to the throne of England. The whole country, even the world, recognized that he was someone special. He was Royalty. His life was destined to be different from others because he is to be different. Long before he was born, everything was put into place that would prepare him to accept his calling as King.

In order for William to be King, he needed to have certain qualities of character that would blossom forth when he took the throne. Special attention would be given to his education, manners, diet, his formed worldview, his vision, his spiritual life, the understanding of his mission and his relationship with those he would one day rule. Consideration would be given to those whom he would choose as friends, companions and advisors. His tutors would be chosen with great care.

WHAT IF, however, immediately after he was born, he was whisked away to some far off country whose culture was completely different, totally opposite to that of England?

And WHAT IF, when was 8 or 13, or 18, or 28 years old (age makes no difference) it was discovered that he was indeed the heir to the throne of England?

He would immediately be taken back to England, loved and accepted by all. However, it would be discovered, that by his character and actions, he is not prepared to mount the steps to the throne. He is a citizen by birth but that in itself does not prepare him to rule and reign. He knows nothing of his mission, has no vision, does not know of the authority that is his and has not heard the call upon his life. He knows nothing of the humility and the sacrifice required; for the honor, that is his.

AS BELEIVERS, we are very much like this stolen child. We were stolen but now are redeemed. And just as the William above needed to be changed from the inside out, we too need this transformation process to take place in our lives if we are to have Christ formed in us. We are to be changed into the very image of Christ – for that is what qualifies us for the throne; the throne? Yes, because we destined to rule and reign with Christ.

Liberty is a not License

We have discussed previously the term internal cross and how it is often overlooked. We concluded that, for man to have fellowship with the Father, he must have within him, the same heart of love that is characterized by the cross. We saw that the journey to the Father's grand plan can only be realized when the Internal Cross becomes a reality in our lives.

In order to progress toward the throne, we must understand the "New Life" that must be allowed to mature within us. That new life is "His Life", the life of Christ. It is a life of righteousness.

How is it that the natural man is dead in trespasses and sins? To find the answer we need to go back to the garden and find Adam. Adam was faced with a choice. He could be totally dependent on God or he could become self-reliant, self-sufficient and totally independent. Since God had made Adam in his own image, he had the ability to decide for himself. He had experienced a dependence upon God since his day of creation and his assessment of all that God had done was that "it was good". However, Satan enters the garden and suggests that Adam could find more enjoyment, more self- fulfillment if he went it alone.

Satan convinced Adam, if he ate of the tree of knowledge of good and evil, he would have the freedom to explore life and be able to express himself in ways not before possible. Since Adam had the ability to think, feel, understand, love, and could express himself with authority (naming the creatures) he surmised, with Satan's help, that he did not need God. Consequently, he made a decision and that decision resulted in him becoming dead in trespasses and sins. God did not create Adam to live by his soul alone and this is where Adam made his error.

I was in Poland when it was under communist rule and witnessed firsthand the oppression they suffered. I witnessed the psychological affect it had on them. They wanted freedom but they also needed a leader who could show them how to live as a free people. When The Berlin Wall fell in the late 1980's, I recall thinking, what are these people going to do with their newfound freedom. They don't know how to be free.

We have read of people in Africa that were suddenly freed from their oppressors, but then just ran around stealing and doing all kinds of crazy things. They had always been told what to do, when to do it and how to do it. They did not know how to think for themselves. They thought that their newfound freedom meant License, allowing them to do whatever they wanted. They knew nothing of responsibility and accountability.

Unlike the above examples, Adam had known what it was to be free. God placed Adam in the Garden of Eden as a FREE moral agent. He was Free to serve whomever, his creator or self. It was his choice. He let Satan deceive him and he made the choice to serve self, which put him under the dominion of Satan.

We were born in sin and under bondage. Therefore, spiritually, like the people of Poland and Africa, we don't know what it is to be free either. When Christ sets us free from sin and death, this is a new experience for us. We don't know what to do with our newfound freedom. We too have a choice to serve a man centered religion or serving a God who so loved us that he gave Himself for us that we might have life and that more abundantly. When a slave is freed, his freedom is his to give away.

Freedom is a Transition Point

Man has misunderstood the concept of freedom. He sees his freedom as a means for self-centeredness instead of seeing it as something that is his to give away. The purpose of the finished work of Christ on Calvary is to provide for the liberation of every man. In this liberation, man is now able to choose to live under a new rule; to be a love-slave unto God or a captive under the Law.

Well then, shall we keep on sinning so that God can keep on showing us more and more kindness and forgiveness?

Of course not! Should we keep on sinning when we don't have to? For sin's power over us was broken when we became Christians and were baptized to become a part of Jesus Christ; through his death the power of your sinful nature was shattered. Your old sin-loving nature was buried with him by baptism when he died; and when God the Father, with glorious power, brought him back to life again, you were given his wonderful new life to enjoy.

For you have become a part of him, and so you died with him, so to speak, when he died; and now you share his new life and shall rise as he did. Your old evil desires were nailed to the cross with him; that part of you that loves to sin was crushed and fatally wounded, so that your sin-loving body is no longer under sin's control, no longer needs to be a slave to sin; for when you are deadened to sin you are freed from all its allure and its power over you. And since your old sin-loving nature "died" with Christ, we know that you will share his new life. TLB." (Rom. 6:1-8).

There are some who can't wait to retire, win the lottery, inherit a lot of money, or find buried treasure. To these people the above all represent freedom. But the statistics tell us that, even though these examples mean freedom, the people who acquire their treasure become slaves to it. We will invite further slavery as we attempt to keep this freedom for ourselves. *"To whom ye yield your members, his servant are you?"* (Gal. 5:1).

If we desire true freedom, we will seek first the Kingdom of God and His Righteousness. It is within the Kingdom of God that we find real liberty and when we do, we will invest our freedom by yielding to Jesus Christ.

---

[1] *Unger's Bible Dictionary, The New Unger's Bible Dictionary,* (Moody Press of Chicago, Illinois. Copyright © 1988

Chapter Fourteen

The Narrow Gate
The Difficult Way

Living with a New Vision

Jesus said, *"Enter by the narrow gate; for wide is the gate and broad is the way that leads to destruction, and there are many who go in by it. Because narrow is the gate and difficult is the way which leads to life, and there are few who find it.* (Matt. 7:13-14).

Jesus was bringing them to a *defining moment* when they had had to decide which Way they would take: the Broad Way or the Narrow Way. He is bringing us to that same defining moment.

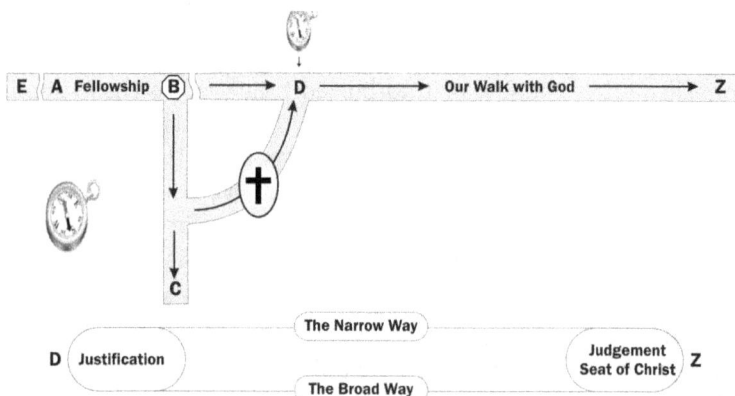

E | A Fellowship (B) ⟶ D ⟶ Our Walk with God ⟶ Z

C

D | Justification

The Narrow Way

The Broad Way

Judgement Seat of Christ | Z

This verse is all too often applied to the unbeliever, but Jesus is here speaking to the believer. Even believers have a difficult time in making this decision to take the Narrow Way. However, we must walk in the way if we are to avoid Satan from stealing, killing or destroying the faith that the Son of God has died to bring to us.

Jesus comes to reclaim and to re-establish His Kingdom. He comes into the midst of the kingdoms of this earth and His purpose is to call out a people from the world unto Himself. His desire is to paint a picture of His Father's kingdom. In this sermon, He is giving the Holy Spirit truths that He can use to penetrate the hearts of those in sound of His voice.

Jesus began by telling the people to repent, have a change in their thinking regarding the Kingdom because it is at hand. He then preached this beautiful message; we call it the Sermon on the Mount. He started with giving eight statements that we refer to as the Beatitudes. He begins by explaining the character that those in the kingdom should exhibit; the character of its citizens.

To understand what Jesus was talking about we must understand the meaning of "character". We are known to others either by observation or by reputation. What is revealed is how we conduct ourselves in various situations and circumstances. What is seen (when there is no pretense) is the real you. Others will see if there is a moral and ethical quality in what you do. In other words, "we do because of who we are".

Jesus then went on to explain the culture of the kingdom that was to be accepted and lived-out by the citizens. Throughout the Sermon on the Mount, Jesus made it perfectly clear that the culture of His Kingdom is thoroughly different from anything they have ever heard or read. It is above all that they could ever think or imagine. That is why He must take the time to, not only describe the character of those who are to be a part of His Kingdom but also tells them how the world will react to them once they come into His Kingdom. By coming into His Kingdom, they must separate themselves from the ways of the world. They are to be in the world but not part of the world. They are to be salt and light to this world.

Jesus elaborated on what they already knew and explained the greater requirement of righteousness that exceeds the Scribes and Pharisees. Jesus turned their thinking upside down when He gave them insight into the truths about giving, praying and fasting. His teaching on the Law regarding murder, divorce, and adultery go way beyond anything they have ever heard before. The demands of the Kingdom must have caused great bewilderment, confusion and for some, disbelief.

He talked in detail about their relationship with God the Father. He described how they were to live in the world and yet, at the same time, live in the presence of the Father. Before He was through, He covered all aspects of life in the Kingdom.

One thing is perfectly clear; we cannot be citizens in both kingdoms or be a part of two cultures. Paul says it plainly to the Church in Corinth, *"Come out from among them and be separate, says the Lord. Do not touch what is unclean, and I will receive you." 'I will be a Father to you, and you shall be My sons and daughters, says the Lord Almighty."* 2 Cor 6:17-18

As a Master Teacher, Jesus stops for a moment and gives His hearers time to reflect on what they have just heard. He is calling for a decision but unless they comprehend, they will not be willing to make a break with the world. They must take time to examine their attitudes in general and their disposition toward the teaching just presented. As the margins on the page of a book give the reader time to digest what is read, time must be given between the stimulus (His words) and the response (their decision) because it will change their lives for an eternity. Will they go the way of the narrow way that leads to abundant life or the broad way that leads to destruction?

What Jesus was saying was, "There is no point in listening further to this sermon; there is no purpose in having followed me through all this (explanation and description) of the Christian Life, if you are not going to take it to heart. What are you going to do about it?"

He has offered them a choice; the religious system they are now living under (slaves to the law) or an opportunity to come into His Kingdom (living as citizens). For us to make a good decision we need to ask ourselves three questions:

- What is my reaction to what I have read in the Bible and in the pages of this book I am reading?

- Am I willing to accept Christ's offer? Many have heard His sermon but have not let it have its way in their heart. They are not ready yet to go through that narrow gate. Let it be known, however, that it is not praise in a song service that Jesus is asking for, but a life lived out in obedience. It is not what a tree looks like that matters: it is by the taste of the fruit that it bears.

- How will I react when the natural disasters, financial collapse and loss of personal freedoms come and beat against my house? How will I react when my own personal world as well as the world around me is no longer what it used to be ? Do I trust in the King?

In other words, our interest in The Sermon on the Mount is useless and valueless, unless we take hold of the truths within it. These truths will enable us to stand during the darkest and most critical hours of our lives.

The Sermon on the Mount is not to be taken piecemeal and understood with the mind. Religious people are always being sidetracked in the details of the message or remain centered on the things that interest them. This is a false approach, which is sharply dividing the people of America into two different camps. This approach to Scripture is what will cause chaos and crisis in the coming days ahead.

If the Church is to demonstrate to the world the culture of the Kingdom of God, we must stand at the Mountain Top and view this sermon from the Lord's perspective. From where He sits, He sees that life in the Kingdom is a result of following Jesus down the Pathway that has been revealed to us by the Holy Spirit.

Christ and the Beatitudes

The Beatitudes have everything to do with the character of the citizens of the Kingdom. Since His disciples knew nothing of what was expected from them as citizens of the Kingdom of God, Jesus takes the opportunity to paint this portrait for all to see.

They are a description of the heart. Even though believers are a new creature in Christ, they still need to deal with the flesh. It is not just the mind that must be transformed but also the heart must submit itself to God.

We are created in the image and likeness of God but when Adam rebelled, he lost that image and dominion. Therefore, the full mission of Jesus not only includes restoring man into

115

fellowship but also making it possible for believers to be transformed into the image of Christ. This is absolutely necessary in order for them to become sons and be able to reign with Him in His Kingdom.

It is because of the new kingdom character formed in them that the culture of His kingdom can be produced in their homes, in the Church and then extended throughout the whole earth.

- *And that you put on the new man which was created according to God, in true righteousness and holiness* Eph. 4:24
- *And have put on the new man who is renewed in knowledge according to the image of Him who created him,* (Col. 3:10)

The Beatitudes are clothed in mystery because they are to be desired by the spirit of the new man not the old man. They are to sought after to be a part of the Christians life not by the working of "self", but by the workings of the Holy Spirit.

The Beatitudes are the basis for ALL of the admonitions given by Paul and Peter to "Put on and Put off". These are the foundation stones of the Christian Life, the life of an Overcomer. The Sermon on the Mount is a complete description of the culture of the Kingdom of Heaven to be lived out by its citizens.

The Kingdom Life

The first thing we notice is that the Kingdom Life is a life to be entered only through a narrow gate. It is not a way of life that is, at first broad and then gets narrower. No! The gate itself is narrow. It is not entered without first having received forgiveness and being reconciled with the Father. There is only one way to the Father and that is through Jesus Christ. Those that just accept Jesus as their savior and then go on to live their life as before know nothing about the narrow gate.

From a standpoint of evangelism, knowing of Kingdom life is essential. When we help people come to a decision to submit to the Lordship of Christ and then leave them to think that this is all there is, we do them a big disservice. The gate is not narrow and then gets less restrictive. All too often, we give the impression that the Christian life is not very different from being a non-Christian. The Christian Life is exciting. It is wonderful. It is an abundant life. However, it is also a narrow way of life. The gate is narrow and so is the way. It is Kingdom living. The pathway is chosen for us. We cannot decide to take another pathway and expect to get to the same destination.

The Christian Life is not just difficult at the beginning; it continues to be difficult. The Christian life is narrow from the beginning to the end. We are in error if we think that it starts narrow, hard, and difficult and then gets easier as we continue. The fight of faith goes right on through life to the end. There will be foes and enemies attacking you right until the very last minute. Because it is this way, *"There are few that find it"*.

There are things that we must leave outside the gate. We must leave behind the crowd, the life of worldliness. We must realize that in the Christian life, we become something exceptional and unusual. The Christian life is not very popular. Nevertheless, it is extraordinary, exceptional, strange, and it is different.

Paul, in his letters, has made it clear what this new life of Christ is to be like. In Colossians 3, he spells it out for us so that we will have no misunderstanding.

- *If therefore ye have been raised with the Christ, seek the things [which are] above, where the Christ is, sitting at [the] right hand of God: have your mind on the things [that are] above, not on the things [that are] lon the earth; for ye have died, and your life is hid with the Christ in God. When the Christ is manifested who [is] our life, then shall ye also be manifested with him in glory.* (Vs. 1)

Paul tells us to *put to death*, in verse 4, the things that belonged to our old nature: *fornication, uncleanness, vile passions, evil lust, and unbridled desire, which is idolatry.* The people that commit these things will not inherit the Kingdom of God. It is because of people doing these things, that the wrath of God is coming.

He then goes on to say in verse 5, *put off or put away* things that must not a part of your new nature in Christ but are a part of your flesh; *wrath, anger, malice, blasphemy, vile language out of your mouth. Do not lie to one another, having put off the old man with his deeds.*

117

The Narrow Gate -The Difficult Way

He is speaking to them and now to us, about the flesh. The things that have become a part of our daily living, those things that have become a part of our lifestyle, our culture and those things that are contrary to what He just had spoke; they cannot continue.

We need to leave "self" outside the gate. We must "put off" as Paul instructs us. They are not a part of Kingdom culture. There must be the working of the internal cross that we have already discussed and about which the Holy Spirit has been dealing with us if we are to enjoy the benefits of living in Christ's Kingdom.

Why is this so important? Verse 1 says we are raised with Christ in newness of life. We have Christ's life within us. We are to yield (surrender, give-up) our self-life in order that His life may live in us. We are to seek the things that are in the Kingdom of Heaven, where Christ sits on His throne next to His Father. So be mindful of the life Christ has available for you in the Kingdom.

By living this new life here on earth, you are bringing the Kingdom of God to the place where you live physically. You're then experiencing, *"Thy Kingdom come on earth as it is in heaven."* There is only one way to live this new life, and it requires that we go through the narrow gate and travel the difficult way.

You can go and join a monastery but still have the way of the World within you. Living the way of the World and the life of the World in a different setting does not make you a Christian nor is it living the life of a Christian.

Jesus said the gate is narrow way and the way is hard because it is. It is not an easy life. Someone has asked if the Christian life is difficult; he answered, "No, it is impossible".

It cannot be lived in the power of self. The standard set by Christ in the Sermon on the Mount is high. Thank God, that it is difficult. It is only a weak person, which wants it easy and wants to avoid the difficult.

The Christian Life is not an ordinary, everyday, run of the mill life. Anybody can do that; but the moment you want to do something unusual, or reach for the heights, you will find that there are not many trying to do the same.

118

The narrow life is a life of giving, and if truly lived, it will involve persecution. The World has always persecuted the man that pursues after righteousness. It is so now and it may be even more so in the last days before Christ's return. Let us then strengthen our inner man that we may be able to stand. *"Now the Spirit expressly says that in latter times some will depart from the faith, giving heed to deceiving spirits and doctrines of demons, speaking lies in hypocrisy, having their own conscience seared with a hot iron,"* (1 Tim. 4:1-3). But the promise is, as we follow this narrow way, we will enjoy the fellowship of His Sufferings.

The recommendation of the broad way is the ease with which it is walked and the great amount of people found along its path. It is as if they are flowing down stream, carried by the current. The natural inclinations are not crossed and they have no interest in rowing upstream. The one disadvantage of this course of action is its end; it leads to destruction.

The end without Christ is a far worse end. Our Lord Himself spoke those parables about the foolish who did not count the cost—the man who started to put up a tower without counting the cost and so had to leave his building unfinished. The same is true of the king who went to fight another king, without assessing the strength of the enemy.

The Lord tells us to count the cost and to face what we have to do before we start. He shows us the whole of life. He has not merely come to save us from punishment and from hell; he has come to make us holy and to purify unto Himself a peculiar people, a family of sons who are zealous of good works.

The Judgment Seat of Christ

Notice again our diagram at the beginning of this Chapter. It shows that at the end of our journey there appears before us the Judgment Seat of Christ. Since we have pointed out that at the end of our days here on earth we shall stand at the Judgment Seat of Christ, a word about this great event is appropriate.

What might be interesting to point out is that everyone (the believer and unbeliever) will get to go to Heaven. Jeremiah 17:10 and 32:19 teach us that every member of the human race will be held accountable, *"according to his ways, according to the fruit of his doings."* The judgment of the unbelievers will be before the Great White Throne described in Revelation 20:15 but the judgment of the Believers will before the Judgment Seat of Christ.

Regarding the Believer, this is also foretold in 2 Corinthians 5:10-11, *"For we must all appear before the judgment seat of Christ, that each one may receive the things done in the body, according to what he has done, whether good or bad. Knowing, therefore, the terror of the Lord, we persuade men; but we are well known to God, and I also trust are well known in your consciences."* That "ALL believers will be judged" will show to all creation, the justice of our God.

Sometime between the resurrection of the dead along with the Rapture of the Church and the personal return of Christ at the Second Advent, every 'born again' believer will stand before the Judgment Seat of Christ. They will be judged for their works and receive their rewards. The Bible says we MUST appear; NO exceptions.

Our standing before the Judgment Seat of Christ instead of the Great White Throne was settled when we were 'born again'. Our sin was judged 'in Christ'. He took all our sin upon Himself and He took the entire penalty for our sin upon Himself as well.

The purpose of the judgment is to determine the value, the worthiness or the worthlessness of our works; those things we've done. Why is this so? Is it because we have been saved unto Good Works? Jesus will judge the motivation as well as the quality of our works.

'Good Works' are produced by walking in Fellowship with God and by being led or controlled by the Holy Spirit. Good Works are not produced by the power of man or within man but only by the power of God. The Fruit of the Spirit will be sought for among your good works. If there are no goods works found or if they do not measure up to the standard, then your labor has been in vain. Do you remember the cursing of the Fig tree?

Believers will gain or lose rewards that are a result of their 'works'. We do not want to be ashamed or have to hang our head low when we stand before Christ. Who among us does not want to hear, *"Well done good and faithful servant"* when we approach Christ's judgment seat?

The rewards that are to be given out are not to bolster the servant's ego but to bring praise and glory to the King, who alone has made the good works possible. Good Works are the fruit of righteousness and they therefore will bring glory to the one who has imputed righteousness.

The rewards are revealed as crowns that we will cast at the feet of Jesus. There is the Crown of Life, The Crown of Righteousness, The Crown of Glory, and The Crown of Rejoicing.

God the Father is now calling out a people (The Church) that He might present them unto the Lord Jesus at the great marriage day of the Lamb. God is now preparing Christ's bride for this great celestial presentation. *"And to her was granted that she should be arrayed in fine linen, clean and white: for fine linen is the righteousness of saints."* WOW! What a day that will be!

The Bride will wear two garments that day.[1] The inner garment, that Christ gives us, and the outer garment, the weaving of our own good works. There is the inner garment of righteousness that comes to those that have received justification by faith. The inner garment is something that God bestows upon us when He washes our sins away and when we wash our robes (our souls) through the washing of regeneration and renewing of the Holy Spirit; He makes them white in the blood of the lamb.

There is also the outer garment of our own obedience to the mandates and commandments of our Lord. The outer garment is the deeds by which we do acts of faith to glorify the name of our Savior. The outer garment is that which we shall wear and it is woven by our own hands. It is made up of those things we have done that our Lord may glorified.

This is the point now to take note of; Paul writes in First Corinthians 3:11-16 that ALL believers will stand before the Judgment Seat of Christ. As we stand before Christ in Heaven, our works will be tried as if by fire. If our works are wood, hay and stubble, they are burned; they are destroyed. If they are gold, silver, and precious stones; they abide as an adornment for the beautiful wedding garment we shall wear when we are presented to the lamb, *"...for his wife has made herself ready."*

Some of us will have on beautiful garments at the marriage. All the good things we have done in the name of Jesus and the works by which we have dedicated a holy life to the Savior; these will make up our garments that sparkle like the jewels of heaven and will be our rewards given at the precious hands of Jesus. However, some of us are going to be practically naked, *"saved as by fire."* All their works will be burned up, all of them. Some of the things that these Christians do will be counted as nothing but worthless. These saints will come to the Marriage of the Lamb with nothing on but the inner garments. Is it any wonder then that Paul pleads with us, *"Therefore, my beloved brethren, be you steadfast, unmovable, always abounding in the work of the Lord, forasmuch as you know that your labor is not in vain in the Lord."* (1 Cor. 15:58).

The garments will belong to you forever. What will you be wearing?

---

[1] C.A. Criswell, *Expository Sermons on Revelation*, preached while Senior Pastor at First Baptist Church, Dallas, TX, 1944-1994

Chapter Fifteen

A Citizen's Life

The Narrow Way

The road to the throne room is through a narrow gate and follows the difficult way. The Beatitudes, given by Jesus, set apart the person who has fully understood the character of a citizen and Grand Plan that the Father has for His children. They are the means (the strait gate and narrow way) that Jesus is referring.

Beatitudes are more than nice sayings: they reveal the very nature of Christ Himself and therefore, the nature of the Citizens of His Kingdom. General characteristics regarding the Beatitudes:[1]

- ALL Christians are to have these characteristics revealed in their life.

- ALL Christians are to manifest ALL of these characteristics. Each of the eight Beatitudes do not stand on their own. Each builds on the other and demands the other. The Beatitudes are a complete whole and you cannot divide them, even though some may be more recognizable than others may. The Beatitudes as a whole must become "internal" in us.

- None of the Beatitudes are what we might call "natural" predisposition. These are spiritual qualities not natural traits. Nobody by birth is like a Christian. The Beatitudes are the result of the work of the Holy Spirit. They amplify the character of Christ within us.

- The Beatitudes are - the essential, utter differences between the Christian and the non-Christian. They are the "WAYS" of God.

The clearer the distinction between the Christian and non-Christian, the greater the effect the Church has on the world. The glory of the Gospel is that when the Church is profoundly different from the world; the world is attracted to it. When we are more like Christ – the more we are unlike those that are not Christian.

Disciples of Christ are different:

A. Different in what they hold in high regard.

B. Different in what they desire and what they seek

C. Different in their Life style

D. Different in what they set out to accomplished

To the Christian, this world is but a proving ground that leads into something vast, eternal and glorious. Peter describes the Christian as a "Pilgrim". We are not talking here of leaving earth for Heaven, but of the Kingdom of God that is within us.

Jesus, the King, spoke these words that we might, not just *have* a relationship, but *enjoy* our fellowship with Him and His Father. He wants us to have an "abundantly life" experience with the Godhead, (Father, Son, and Holy Spirit). This dynamic fellowship with the Godhead can only happen when we are manifesting the life of Christ as expressed in the Beatitudes.

The Sermon on the Mount, of which the Beatitudes are a part, does not give the plan of salvation for the Captive. It gives a way of life that is to be embraced by the children of God here on Earth. It is given to those that have responded to Jesus' invitation to repent and receive the forgiveness of God and follow Him.

Those hearing the message for the first time had come from a Jewish upbringing that had emphasized the adherence to the Law. Jesus is now teaching them the true nature of righteousness and what is the true character of those that belong to Him.

"Blessed are the poor in Spirit for theirs is the kingdom of heaven."

Jesus did not say poor in attitude, outlook, position or money. He said poor in spirit. He is concerned about the quality of our spirit's character. The kingdom is not for the proud but for those that cry out for mercy. No one cries out for mercy unless they feel the pain of their sin, the hurt that they have caused others and the consequences of their actions. It is for those that put their hand into their pockets looking for goodness and find –

nothing. It is not for the religious but for those that know that their righteousness is as filthy rags. It is for those who see their nakedness and shame as they stand before the King of the Universe. It is only those who; are "poor in spirit" that will mourn, be led by the Spirit, hunger and thirst for righteousness, be merciful, be pure in heart, be a peacemaker, and be willing to be persecuted for righteousness sake.

"Blessed are those that mourn, for they shall be comforted."

There is no rejoicing when you are mourning. Mourning passes after time when you lose a loved one, go through a divorce, lose a job, or go through some other traumatic experience. However, there is no real comfort that can be given by man; whether it is fame, fortune, or worldly pleasure when a man is convicted of his sin. The only thing that will satisfy (comfort) his soul is the forgiveness of God, given to him when he repents. As Jesus cried over Jerusalem, it should not be for our sin alone but all those still in darkness that we mourn.

"Blessed are the meek for they shall inherit the earth."

Those that will inherit the earth – not heaven- are those that have proven themselves to be able to rule and reign with Christ. The meek are those that embrace the "internal Cross" and are led by the Holy Spirit. The meek will do exploits for their King because; it is not by power nor by might that we shall reign, but by the Spirit. Heretofore, the Holy Spirit has been working to effect a change in us now He seeks to lead and empower us. (See Meekness on page 132).

"Blessed are those that hunger and thirst after righteousness for they shall be filled."

The depth and breathe of our fellowship with the King is determined by the depth and breathe of the righteousness of Christ revealed in us. To those that see themselves as starving, empty and in need of nourishment, Jesus says to them, *"I am the Bread of Life". "If any man comes to me, I will give him living water."* The starving and thirsty can think of nothing else but to find food and drink; so it is for those that are thus concerned about their soul. David in Psalm 23 says of his God, *"He prepares a table for me in the presence of mine enemies; my cup runs over. Surely goodness and mercy shall follow me all the days of my life."*

"Blessed are the merciful for they shall obtain mercy."

You cannot give what you have not received. Those that show mercy are those who have received mercy. God has shown His mercy by holding back His anger and wrath because of our sin. He did not let his anger control him but let His love rule in His heart and in His actions. Those that are merciful have experienced His forgiveness and His Holy Spirit has filled their heart with love that they may show that same love to others. Now they respond to others as Jesus did because mercy is part of their spirit nature.

"Blessed are the pure in heart for they shall see God."

When we consider metals and minerals; the purer (without contaminates) they are, the more they are valued. These pure metals are the more costly because they have gone through a refining process. In the process, they tumble against each other to knock off the worthless material, and then they are washed and put through the fire until all the impurities are burnt away. Like jewels in a crown, it is only the purest that are fit for a King. Therefore, it is, only those, that go through the refiner's fire, that will ever enjoy the deepest fellowship of the King. It is no wonder that these people are called blessed. *"Who may ascend into the hill of the Lord? Or who may stand in His holy place? He who has clean hands and a pure heart."* (Ps. 24:3-4).

"Blessed are the peacemakers for they shall be called the sons of God."

It takes faith and courage to step into the middle of a fight because in the process, you could be injured. It takes you from the sidelines and puts you into the arena. Those that are Peacemakers not only have faith and courage but also have compassion and authority. Those that step into the fight are confident of the victory. The peacemaker is not concerned with the feelings of the aggressor but is concerned with the helplessness and hopelessness of the victim. They use their authority to command and use their faith and compassion to bring deliverance, healing, and peace to the oppressed.

"Blessed are those who are persecuted for righteousness sake,
for theirs is the kingdom of heaven."

In a cruel and wicked society, the righteous will stick out like a sore thumb when compared to those that are evil and love the darkness. When the righteous appear, the light has come. The wicked do not want their deeds exposed because they are evil. Those that are righteous are not persecuted because they are sitting in their homes, in their churches, or hanging out with their Christian friends. They are persecuted because they are out in the marketplace, challenging the sinners to examine themselves to see if there is any good in them. They know that, as the evil people examine themselves, the Holy Spirit will find an opportunity to convict of sin, righteousness and judgment. It is because of this that they are persecuted. Jesus said, *"If they hated me, they will hate you".*

Stepping Stones to a New Life

We can use these characteristics to paint a portrait of a Christian. The Beatitudes, in reality, are a portrait of Jesus as He walks among men today within us. They are a portrait of our God because Hebrews says that Jesus is the express image of the Father.

These eight beatitudes reveal the Christian at his/her very best. What we must recognize is that these characteristics are revealed only as the Holy Spirit has brought them forth and transformed the Christian.

The Holy Spirit works in an orderly manner; therefore, there is a definite order of the Beatitudes. They are not placed haphazardly or by chance. There is a spiritual, logical sequence to their placement.

We stated it at the beginning and we will continue to state it: it is all about relationship! You cannot begin to take into your spirit these eight Beatitudes without a relationship with the Holy Spirit.

We begin our new life in Christ with the Holy Spirit convicting us of sin, righteousness and judgment. He, the Holy Spirit, is at work, and continues transforming us into the image of Christ. There is nothing done for us, in us, and through us,

127

that is not the work of the Holy Spirit. He is transforming us into the very image of Jesus Christ, our Lord and Savior.

Churchgoers today are coming from all occupations and lifestyles. They are coming from cultures that know nothing of Christianity as a relationship. They are from another religious background or are from a culture that has no religion at all. They know nothing of the culture of the Kingdom.

Wherever they are from, they are looking for a way through life. They are not sure where they are going or how to get there; however, they are looking for fulfillment, peace, joy and freedom. They want to put the puzzle of life together but don't have a picture of what it looks like. They are looking for secure stones on which step in order to advance toward fulfilling their purpose.

Whenever we see our destination as something wonderful, exciting and something to be desired we become focused and alive with anticipation. The destination that God offers us is a relationship. A relationship that holds out a promise that one day we will joint heirs with Christ in the kingdom of God.

There is a peace, joy, and excitement within when you know where you are going and how to get there. You can focus on the journey and enjoy the ride, even if it filled with bumps and difficulties along the way. The hardships of the journey do not get you down nor do they dampen your spirits because the reward is ever before you.

A Study on the First Three Beatitudes

"BLESSED ARE THE POOR IN SPIRIT FOR THEIRS IS THE KINGDOM OF HEAVEN."

Why is this Beatitude first? There is no entry into the Kingdom apart from being "poor in spirit". There is no one in the Kingdom who is not "poor in spirit". It is the "strait gate", the fundamental characteristic of the citizen of the Kingdom. It begins with self-examination.

The Kingdom of God is a kingdom founded on Righteousness and Justice, which is why Jesus said to Nicodemus, "*Most assuredly, I say to you, unless one is born again, he cannot see the Kingdom of God."* John 3:3

What it is:

- Feeling nothing less than utter poverty of righteousness in the Presence of God
- Spiritual Brokenness
- Knowing that we cannot bring about righteousness ourselves by being "good" or through "good works"
- It is utter our dependence upon God and obeying God's highest commands
- It is the work of the internal cross, John 12: 24-26
- It is Humbleness to its extreme

Illustrations from Scripture:

Jesus: Phil. 2:5-8	Paul: Phil. 3:13
Jacob: Gen. 32:10	Moses: Exod. 3:11
Gideon: Judges 6:15	David: 2 Sam. 7:18
Solomon: 1 Kings. 3:7	Centurion: Matt. 8:18
Paul: 1Tim. 1:1	Peter: Luke. 5:8-9

What it is not:

- Contrasting ourselves with others
- Retiring
- Weak
- Lacking in Courage
- self-effacing
- Staying in the background
- Dressing like a nobody
- Repressing true personality
- "I'm a no account"
- "I'm just a sinner saved by grace"
- Relying on traits that I'm responsible for

A Citizen's Life

This is the first principle that is required in the thought process of the Christian. When a Holy God confronts a person who is Poor in spirit, they realize that they have nothing that can satisfy God's demand for justice; they find no righteousness within. We are all as naked before God with nothing in our hand that can erase our sin. There is nothing we can do to make ourselves clean. Our righteousness is as filthy rags. Our wickedness stands out like cow manure on a dinner table. There is nothing we have that can hide it or cover the smell. We must accept God's offer of a covenant of peace or suffer the consequences. We must accept His promise that He will put within us a "new" spirit.

"BLESSED ARE THOSE THAT MOURN FOR THEY SHALL BE COMFORTED."

The World wants nothing to do with mourning. It finds enough sadness in everyday life. The world shuns mourning – 'Forget your troubles and do all you can to hide from your troubles'. Escapism becomes a way of life. Jesus impresses upon us that ONLY those that *do* mourn are happy. Jesus condemns the happiness of this world, *"Woe unto you that laugh now, for you shall mourn and weep."* (Luke 6: 21).

There is a natural mourning – death of a loved one, loss of a home by fire or hurricane, loss of a job. But even these are of varying degrees (scale of 1-10).

Spiritual Mourning follows "Poor in Spirit". As I am confronted by God and His Holiness and contemplate the life I am meant to live in His Kingdom; I see my utter helplessness. I discover my emptiness of spirit and immediately that makes me mourn. I MUST MOURN! As a man examines himself – he must mourn for his sins, not just for the things he does but also for who he is capable of doing. (See 1 Cor 11: 27-32).

The mourning that Jesus is concerned with here is as it affects our character. It is spiritual. It is an attitude NEVER found in the world. It is mourning over our sin in thought, words and deeds. This mourning produces more than "I'm sorry". It produces a deep sorrow that causes us to seek for forgiveness and to change our ways.

130

The mourning that we are trying to describe is such that it sees not only the consequences of ungodliness but also the rewards of holiness. It sees a life unable to please a holy God as well as a life full of Joy that results from a heart moved to mourn. The mourning we are trying to describe is demonstrated by Jesus as He cries, not only over the lost, but also because He is moved to seek and to save those that are lost.

In every revival, the Church attracts the world ONLY as it functions as being "Christ-like". This Beatitude then does have a great effect on matters of evangelism. We can reference the Welch Revival of 1901; bars shut down for lack of customers, police found nothing to do – there was no crime and families became families again.

Two reasons why the Church has not been effective as it relates to this Beatitude:

Reason # 1--The Church's failure to understand Sin and its consequences. Many in the Church do not understand what sin is and this defective understanding of sin leads to an absence of a sense of Sin. This then leads the Christian to live a life of compromise. When man abandons his dependence on God, he believes he can go it alone. God's way is to lead man to peace and joy. Any other way will result in sin. Man, left to himself, will always end up on the side of God's enemies.

Why do so many have no idea of what constitutes Sin? Why? The World has no idea of what Sin is. Sin has been watered down so that no one recognizes it any more. *Tolerance* and *Compromise* are the Buzzwords for the time in which we live. The Church has been following the World. It does not know what pleases the King of Kings or what grieves the Holy Spirit. It is looking for: "How to be a better me".

A mourning Christian, however, does not judge others but sees their lack of peace within, therefore he mourns for them. He sees the state of our society, our nation, and the World. He is disgusted, he is horrified (this is where the church stops) but he does not stop there; he mourns because of it. He understands what sin means to God – His hatred of it, His abhorrence of it, which causes him to mourn.

Reason # 2-- The Church's failure to understand joy. Lacking understanding of the true nature of Biblical joy has left the Christian community with not much to offer the sinner except a false hope. Real hope is full of joy that is unspeakable and full of glory. There is rejoicing even in the face of adversity. Real joy comes from a right standing with God.

Truth: You must mourn in order to be filled with joy and you must come under conviction before you can be converted. A real sense of sin must come before there can be true joy of salvation.

Some would give anything to find this true joy. The Church building is full of sinners looking for this joy. The Church of today tells them they will find it in Jesus. Just accept Him as your Savior. HOWEVER, they never find this true joy because they never received the truth about; "Blessed are those that mourn, *for it is they and they alone* that will be comforted".

"BLESSED ARE THE MEEK FOR THEY SHALL INHERIT THE EARTH."

The meek Christian is not concerned with himself. He takes the old adage, "Sticks and stones may break my bones but names will never hurt me" to a new level of meaning. He knows how he is to, *"live, move, and have his being"*. He knows who he is. He is a child of the highest God. He is on the road to maturity and is being prepared to sit on the throne with Christ.

He is traveling the difficult way. He is totally dependent on Prayer. He does not assert himself. He does not use his position. His strength is in his obedience and submission to the authority of his King. He is an Ambassador of his King; speaking and acting only on his behalf. The power that he commands is not his. The glory that will be revealed is not his to receive.

What it is:

It is total dependence on God to complete the task.

It is a disposition brought about by the work of the Holy Spirit

It a true view of oneself in attitude and conduct

There is an absence of pride

The meek makes no demands for the position he holds

What it is not:

A person who is by their own effort:

Humble	Unassuming	Submissive	Tame
Gentle	Yielding	Docile	Soft
Modest	Mild	Accepting	Kind
Consenting	Calm	Easy Going	

Examples: the following examples show an aspect of meekness that makes the name of God known. Moses, along with Joshua, Elijah, Elisha, David and others in the Old Testament and New Testament, brought forth miracles and other works of power; not of their own ability, but because of the one they serve. What in their lives made this so and why will it be in ours also? The answer is meekness.

- Since the Meek person is totally dependent on God and is lead by the Holy Spirit; the resources available to him are not limited to himself but rather are unlimited as they are given by God.

- Meekness is for every child of God no matter their calling. It is not just for the Moses' or the Elijah's', it is to be a *characteristic of every Disciple* today.

- Whatever is set before you, whatever the task, whatever the demand, you can do it. You can do it because, it is not you who is doing it but God through you.

Empting the Vessel

What is truly amazing is that Jesus would humble himself to the extent that He (being the Word of God – therefore the same as God) would not use His power as God to further the work of God. Jesus emptied himself (laid aside His mighty power and glory) and became a man, therefore, what allowed Him to do the works of God was this; the working out of meekness. What we see in Jesus is meekness. This meekness in Jesus is the work of the Spirit. Jesus was meek because His dependence was always upon the Holy Spirit and not in His own human ability.[2]

All through the Old Testament, we see men who had a heart for God but could do nothing until the Holy Spirit came upon them and it was then that they were able to do the Works of God. We read of miracle after miracle being done by ordinary men who died to self and allowed God to use them in a supernatural way.

Moses too was called meek, but it took forty years on the backside of the desert to develop it. Sometimes that is what it takes to bring us to a total dependence on the Spirit's power.

Forty years earlier Moses had thought his position, his strength, his education would get the job done but it wasn't until Moses died to self that God was able to use him. As we put the "old man" to death, we are preparing our spirit to be in oneness with the Holy Spirit whereby God can do His work through us.

Being used of God to do the supernatural goes way beyond humility. Humility will cause us to see ourselves as mere men and no better than anyone else. Humility causes the grace of God to come to us. Yes, our God gives grace to the humble and if we sense that we are in the presence of greatness, we humble ourselves. If we are a trumpet player and come into the presence of a great musician we are awed and wouldn't dare to play in his presence least we be embarrassed.

Meekness, even though it involves humility, is not humility. Humility will bring us to our knees and we will cry out. There is no crying out with meekness. With meekness, you have courage and there is no fear of the enemy because of our absolute dependence upon God.

Why is this Beatitude important to God? It was Jesus himself that said, *"The meek shall inherit the earth"*.

In examining The Beatitudes, we see the Spirit working in a man's heart. All of these characteristics are the work of the Holy Spirit and are not inherent in man.

---

[1] D. Martin Lloyd-Jones, Studies in The *Sermon on the Mount,* 1959
[2] Philippians 2:5-7 This is often referred to as "The 'kenosis' of Christ"

Kingdom Insights

Chapter Sixteen

Kingdom Sacraments

The Body Connection

Every Christian Church provides its members or adherents the opportunity to take communion and involve themselves in Water Baptism. Communion and Water Baptism are what connect us to the Community of God in a physical sense. Water Baptism is a one-time act while participating in Communion is an ongoing act, whether it is daily, weekly or monthly.

Jesus stands in the present, with His arms stretched out connecting us to the past and to the future. In both of these Kingdom Sacraments He makes them both personal and corporate.

In Communion, Jesus reaches back to the Passover when the Children of Israel were delivered out of Egypt and then brought into a relationship with Almighty God. He reaches out into the future when He says, *"With fervent desire I have desired to eat this Passover with you before I suffer; for I say to you, I will no longer eat of it until it is fulfilled in the kingdom of God."* Luke 22:15-16

In Water Baptism He takes us back to the crossing of the Red Sea when the Children of Israel walked through the water and came out alive on the other side. He takes us into the future when the Apostle Paul, *"Therefore we were buried with Him through baptism into death, that just as Christ was raised from the dead by the glory of the Father, even so we also should walk in newness of life".* Rom 6:4

Communion

Every time we take Communion, we are affirming that we are remaining faithful to the covenant that we have entered into. As we stand in the midst of the congregation, we are making a statement; that we are in remembrance of the covenant made possible by the broken body and shed blood of Jesus Christ. We are also proclaiming that by the grace of God, we will remain faithful throughout our life to keep our covenant with the King of Glory.

When we eat the broken bread, we are offering our lives as a living sacrifice. We shout that we are willing to die for our King, which is our reasonable service according to Paul. If this truth has not hit you, please stop right now and read *Fox's Book of Martyrs, Tortured for Christ* and Hebrews 11: 35-40.

When we drink from the cup, we are to lift it high for all to see because we are saying, "Long live the King". We proclaim to all that we are giving our allegiance, our loyalty, our hands to hold the sword and our feet to run to the battle in order that our King's kingdom shall be extended throughout the whole earth. Communion is very much personal, yet at the same time, it is also corporate. Communion is not done in a secret place; it is taken together with others that share the same love for Jesus Christ and the same allegiance to the King of kings. We are in relationship with one another.

Paul warns us that we are to examine ourselves before taking communion. It is loyalty, not sin, which we are looking for in our lives. The lack of loyalty will bring about sin. If we look for sin only, it is like missing the forest because of seeing only the trees.

Jesus said, *"Not everyone who says to me, 'Lord, Lord,' will enter the kingdom of heaven, but only he who does the will of my Father who is in heaven. Many will say to me on that day, 'Lord, Lord, did we not prophesy in your name and in your name drive out demons and perform many miracles?' Then I will tell them plainly, 'I never knew you; Away from me, you evildoers!'"* (Matt. 7:21-23).

It is a time that we also allow the Holy Spirit to reveal our hidden sins that we might confess our sin and receive forgiveness. Nothing must be allowed to remain that will hinder our walk with the Lord. The term "Lord" should have special meaning for us wherever it is written in the Bible for it denotes ownership. We have been bought with a price, not silver or gold but with the precious blood of our LORD Jesus Christ. He is our King. Make the Kingdom connection. We are His and He is ours.

Water Baptism

As part of the Great Commission, Jesus commands us to go and make disciples and baptize the new converts. John's baptism was a baptism of repentance; a baptism that says that I have entered into a new way of thinking about the things that I've done. When we go under the water and come up, we are declaring that I once was a thief, adulterer, liar, whatever; but I have changed my thinking toward these things. I now hate these things because they are an abomination to God, I have asked God for forgiveness and I am now a new creature in Christ.

I love what Paul said, *"Do you not know that the unrighteous will not inherit the kingdom of God? Do not be deceived. Neither fornicators, nor idolaters, nor adulterers, nor homosexuals, nor sodomites, nor thieves, nor covetous, nor drunkards, nor revilers, nor extortioners will inherit the kingdom of God. "And such were some of you. But you were washed, but you were sanctified, but you were justified in the name of the Lord Jesus and by the Spirit of our God."* (1 Cor. 6:9-11, emphasis added).

Something else changed for these new converts; they (you and I) are now citizens of the Kingdom of God. We have been translated from the kingdom of darkness into the Kingdom of the Son of God.

In any country that accepts immigrants, these immigrants are given very limited rights. They are given the right to work, drive a car, get an education and live anywhere in the country. However, they must register yearly and renew their green card, allowing them to work.

It is the expectation that each new immigrant would desire citizenship and therefore work toward the enrichment of his or her new country. Citizenship status, under social contract theory, carries with it both rights and responsibilities. "Active citizenship" is the philosophy that citizens should work towards the betterment of their community through economic participation, public service, volunteer work and other such efforts to improve life for all citizens.

Whatever their prior political or cultural position, it is no longer valid in the new country. If you came from Russia and were a communist, that position must be left outside the shores and the constitution of the new adopted country accepted. We must be reminded to keep looking ahead and not look back as Jesus said, *"No one, having put his hand to the plow, and looking back, is fit for the kingdom of God."* (Luke 9:62).

The parallel exists here for the Kingdom of God. The difference is that in becoming a citizen of the Kingdom does not involve a process; it is instantaneous. When we are "born again" we automatically become a citizen of the Kingdom. It is a birth right; Jesus said, "Unless one is "born again" one cannot enter the Kingdom of God".

Foreign nationals who wish to become citizens of the United States may do so through the naturalization process. Citizenship confers many advantages -- the right to vote, protection from the government, access to certain jobs and benefits, and the option to hold public office.

What does all this have to do with Water Baptism?

In Water Baptism, we identify with Christ in His life, death, burial and resurrection; that's personal. However, since it is public in nature, it also signifies a relationship with others that also have identified with Christ in the same manner; we have become members of the household of Faith.

In Water Baptism, there is a death side and a living side; a going down and a coming out of. We often talk about identification with Christ in Water Baptism because we haven't died physically. Yes, not physically but our death to sin is just as real as Christ dying on the Cross of Calvary. Let the words of Paul sink deep into your heart, *"What shall we say then? Shall we continue in sin that grace may abound? Certainly not! How shall we who died to sin live any longer in it? Or do you not know that as many of us as were baptized into Christ Jesus were baptized into His death"?* (Rom. 6:1-3).

We now live because Christ rose from the dead and has life. It is His life that He now freely gives to us who have also died. Paul said it so clearly, *"I have been crucified with Christ; it is no longer I who live, but Christ lives in me; and the life which I now live in the flesh I live by faith in the Son of God, who loved me and gave Himself for me".*

140

(Gal. 2:20-21). This is so important because Christ's Kingdom is a kingdom of Righteousness.

In Romans, Paul admonishes us to walk a new way (a narrow way) when he says, *"Therefore we were buried with Him through baptism into death, that just as Christ was raised from the dead by the glory of the Father, even so we also should walk in newness of life"*. (Rom. 6:4).

This new life of Christ is received when we are 'born again' and means we are justified, which gives us a new position before God. This new position is citizenship in the Kingdom of God. Our citizenship in the Kingdom of God is a badge of highest honor and should be worn proudly. It should be seen by all, 24/7, 365 days, as you live righteously in obedience to your new King.

Church attendance, going to Bible Studies, singing in the choir, being on the evangelism committee or editor of the church newsletter does not show that you now have met the standards or qualifications for citizenship. Only Water Baptism tells others in the Church that you are 'born again', and are going to live a righteous life without hesitation. You are proclaiming that you are now a citizen of the Kingdom of God.

Chapter Seventeen

Kingdom Living

Upside down turned Right side up

In the summer of 1973, shortly after I was 'born again', I had the privilege of attending a Bill Gothard Basic Youth Conflict Seminar. It was held at the Chicago Civic Center where about 5,000 attended. It was a wonderful 5-day event. For me, it was a time of transformation. I had been involved with a mainline church all my life but knew nothing of having a life changing experience. It was truly a Romans 12:1-2 moment in my life, a renewing of my mind by the Word of God. I thank God for that opportunity.

One thing that I was constantly hearing and reading from the Gothard material was, "we must relinquish our rights". We were servants therefore; we had no rights. God was in control and we must let Him have His way. It was said that everything that happened to us was a result of a loving God that was working out His purposes in our life. Gothard referenced the Apostle Paul calling himself a bond slave and Jesus saying that the greatest in the Kingdom is servant to all.

However, there was one thing that troubled me during the months that followed that seminar. Even with all that Jesus said about servanthood, I recalled that Jesus also said in John 15:15, *"No longer do I call you servants, for a servant does not know what his master is doing; but I have called you friends, for all things that I heard from My Father I have made known to you."*

As I read my Bible, it became clear that being 'born again' meant I was part of God's family but it also meant I had become a Citizen of His Kingdom. If I believed this, then what was being revealed was a different mindset from what I had received from Bill Gothard and was more than just being 'Born Again' and going to heaven when I die.

If I was to accept this new premise of 'being a citizen of a Kingdom', then I must conclude that God's original purpose for

His creation was to rule the visible world from the invisible. Because God had given Man a spirit, He could therefore communicate with Man and in effect, live in Man by planting his Word in his heart. Thus, in cooperation with Man, God would extend His heavenly Kingdom to Earth – the invisible ruling the visible, an invisible God ruling through a visible man.

Problem solved with a test

Trying to process these two conflicting mindsets was causing no little turmoil within me. I had to reach a conclusion. I was a King's Kid and a citizen of the Kingdom or I was not. I began reading and studying my Bible more. I read what others were saying on this extraordinarily important subject.

Then one day the test came; our family was driving back from Rochester, NY to Chicago where I was working as a Sales Engineer. We had gone to NY to pick up some bedroom furniture and mattresses. We had put them in the back of our pick-up truck, tied them down, put plastic over them and away we went. Of course, the plastic covering became useless as we drove 65 MPH down interstate 90 and 80.

As we were traveling through Indiana, a huge thunderstorm loomed in front of us. We could see the cars coming toward us with their windshield wipers still running. We could hear the plastic flapping in the wind and all we could think about was the mattresses getting soaked and ruined and what a mess that was going to be.

Although we were getting closer and closer to the rain, we knew not all was lost. We had remembered what we had studied in the Bible, what we had read in books like, "Like a Mighty wind" by Mel Torrey and others who had written stirring accounts of the miraculous power and love of God.

Bea got out our notes and our Bible and began feverishly looking up scriptures that would build our faith and then enable us to take dominion over the situation. Yes, take dominion, just as God had intended for man to do at the beginning and now made possible because Jesus had returned dominion back to those who were redeemed and "Born Again" into the family of God.

As our faith began to increase, we also began to speak it forth and as faith increased so did the peace that only Jesus can give. We knew, that we knew, that the rain would not come near our truck. We came closer and closer to the rain and as we did, the clouds began to part and just as we reached the rain – we could see the rain falling on both the right side and left side of our truck. The only water that hit our truck came from the splash as we drove through the puddles of water on the road.

We were convinced that God's Word was true but God was not done yet. He wanted to make sure this was settled in our heart. Six months later God revealed that He is still in the business of bring forth dreams and visions. One night in January 1974, God gave to me a vision regarding foster children and a house. One year later, we moved into the very house that I saw in the vision with my family and two foster children. To tell of all the miracles that took place along the way would take to long. Nevertheless, it does bring us to the telling of another experience that deals with dominion and visions.

One year later, we moved to Mt Vernon, Ohio. God again had given to me a vision of our home. I went to see the local Real Estate man, Larry Lotz. I told Larry of the house that I had seen in the vision. I knew he was a Believer because when I entered his office he was reading his Bible; one of those that has 4 translations. He closed his Bible and said, "Let's go". He took me straight to the house that I had described to him - in great detail.

Let me tell you a little about Larry. Larry and his wife Caroline had been married for several years without having any children. When Caroline finally did get pregnant, they were the happiest people in the world. When Devin was born, however, their happiness soon turned to utter despair. When they brought Devin home from the hospital, all he did was cry and cry. After two days, they took that little bundle of joy back into the hospital only to discover that Devin was born without any Kidneys. That's right, No kidneys at all! They spent the night at his side with the doctors explaining everything about his condition.

Larry's story

The doctor told Larry and Caroline, "There is nothing anyone can do. The only thing left to do is to go home, get some sleep and ask the One above for help." His brother-in-law, who heard the doctor and feeling helpless himself, came over and said, "Why not ask God to heal him?" The lack of sleep, the heartbreak of Devin's condition and the sadness they saw in each other's face was just too much for them to handle. They left the hospital in tears and drove home.

Larry had gone to church in his younger years but at 18 he left and when he and Caroline got married, going to church was not part of their lifestyle. Larry himself admits that his life of drinking and being a part of the worldly scene did not lend itself to be thinking about God, no matter how bad things were for Devin. Certainly, that night, God did not seem very real to him.

When they got home, while still in the car, Caroline looked at Larry and said, "Larry let's give our lives to God and ask Him to heal Devin". They both cried out to God and told Him they would live only for Him and asked God to heal their son and give him kidneys so he could live.

The next day they went back to the hospital; there had been a changed in Devin's condition. To make a very long story short, the doctor told him that something very unusual had happened. When they examined Devin again, they found that he did indeed have two very healthy kidneys. They could not explain it but there was no denying it and that Devin was healthy enough to go home. God heard their prayer that night and both Larry and Caroline have been living for their King ever since. When I met Devin, he was 5 or 6 years old; that was 25 years ago.

Here is where we get back to the dominion part. Larry, now a Believer and Overcomer, left the church of his family and sought out a Bible believing Church. He and Caroline began to grow in their faith and they read everything he could about this miracle working God that he now knew personally. He too began to understand about the Kingdom of God and our place in it as citizens.

Then his faith was tested.

Larry and his family lived on a small farm in Fredericktown, Ohio. He was not a farmer but he did have some cows and chickens. One day during a storm, a funnel cloud formed just west of his property. He could see that it was coming his way and was about to touch down. Larry didn't have time to search out his Bible for Scriptures regarding Dominion; he didn't need to – he already had them in his heart. As the tornado touched down, he began to use his God given authority and commanded that tornado to bypass his property. He spoke to the storm just as Jesus had done and as I had done a few years earlier in Indiana.

People couldn't believe the story either when Larry told them, but there was no denying the truth when they came out and saw for themselves. The path of the twister ran right up to Larry's farm and then it mysteriously jumped over his property and came down again on the other side to continue on its way.

When your Faith is tested, will you know that your citizenship in the Kingdom of God will have real meaning for you and your family? Why not settle this now, once and for all.

Chapter Eighteen

Kingdom Worldview

The Bedrock for Christian faith

Our worldview, Biblical or not, is a product of our culture. When we talk to some people, who have never given any thought to just anything, and ask them what they think about a particular subject; they, plain and simple, do not make any sense. They are confused because they have never been taught the basics of life. They have lived life on their own and have drawn their conclusions only from their personal experiences. They have never been able to put the puzzle together because they don't have a clue as to what it should look like.

All worldviews, including a Biblical Worldview, must pass certain tests:

1. Is it rational, is it supported by evidence? It should be consistent with what we observe.

2. Does it give a satisfying comprehensive explanation of reality, does it explain why things are the way they are?

3. Does it provide a satisfactory basis for living, therefore, not leaving us to borrow from another worldview?

There are two approaches to a Biblical Worldview. The FIRST approach concludes that the men who wrote the Bible were inspired to varying degrees, but were subject to the limitations of their experiences, worldviews and personal prejudices. Therefore, the Bible is approached in the same manner as any other literature without any presuppositions as to its inspiration. This is the position of many in the Christian community to some degree or another.

It rejects the literal meaning of Scripture because of some mythological language. Its greatest weakness is that it places the basis of its adherent's theology in the realm of the objective and

147

experimental. They say that Scripture must be interpreted within the bounds of scientific evidence. THEREFORE, persons holding this view do not believe in miracles, physical healing or anything supernatural. That person places science above the Word. It is a theology that says, I see therefore, I believe". They judge Scripture by physical evidence rather than allowing Scripture to judge their experience.

This view allows it adherents to believe that Scripture *contains* the Word of God. Therefore, if you are uncertain that the Bible means what it clearly states or if you believe it contains errors and contradictions, THEN it cannot shed its light in or on your life.

John Wesley said, "If there be any mistakes in the Bible, there may as well be a thousand. If it is untrustworthy in one place, it cannot be trusted at all."

The SECOND approach presupposes that the Bible is the Word of God and is inspired by the Holy Spirit. If we assume that God is perfect and cannot make a mistake, and if God inspires the Bible, then the Bible is free from mistakes and contradictions.

Just to blindly believe this, however, would be foolish. If Sarah, Abraham's wife checked out God - See Heb. 11:11, why should not we. She judged Him faithful who had promised. God had been making promises right from the beginning of creation. What Sarah found out through her investigation was that God always kept His promises. He had always kept His Word. He had always been faithful. It was scientific evidence that she judged. She judged the Word of God as it had been spoken to men that came before Abraham. It was HE, the person of God, which she judged. That is the difference. As she checked Him out, her faith turned to confidence.

There are a number of interpretations of Scripture, some people will argue. Some will even go to the point of war for the position they have accepted. Part of the problem can be explained by faulty assumptions and bad exegesis skills as people approach the Bible. However, there can be another reason.

What I have seen over the last 38 years is that we often come to a belief without a revelation from the Holy Spirit. Our conclusions have not come by studying and meditating on the Word but because godly and respected teachers have told us so. We trusted them; however, we have listened to the echoes instead of the voice of God. There is nothing wrong in listening to an echo, if we have come to the same understanding through revelation.

Seven Basic Questions to acquire a complete worldview.[1]

Question One
What is Prime Reality?

In order to accept our Worldview as Biblical we first must look at three assumptions about God as the Cause of all things.

God exists. When we describe God, we attribute to Him five qualities or characteristics. He is *eternal*, He is *all powerful*, He is *everywhere present*, He is *all knowing*, and He is *all Wise*. Because of these attributes, we say that our God and He alone, is the creator and the sustainer of all things. We state that everything that He has made was, "Good". We also ascribe to Him other qualities such as Love, Mercy, Grace, Peace, Joy, Longsuffering, Patient, Good, Kind and Just.

We do not come to this conclusion by empirical evidence; we do not try to prove that there is a God. We do not try to reason upward from ourselves to God. The late Prof. Calderwood of the Edinburgh University observed, "The divine existence is a truth so plain that it needs no proof, as it is a truth so high that it admits of none."[2] In other words, we can just look at His creation and know that someone supernatural had to make it come into being. How it happened we do not know, at first, but a humble heart finds a loving God that reveals Himself.

Hebrews 11:6 "but without faith it is impossible to please him, for he who comes to God must believe that he is. And that he is a reward or of those that diligently seek him."

We can know Him.

God knows that it is impossible for Man on his own to recognize God. So he has sent the Holy Spirit into this world to reveal Himself to Man. All Man has to do is walk around and wonder, who created this; how did it all come about? God would reveal Himself to such a Man. Not only that, God has given to every man a measure of faith to believe in Him. (See Hebrews 11:6 above and Rom 12:3).

Jews and Christians are the only faiths that recognize that their God is a living God and is not a respecter of persons. Growing in understanding of a Prime Reality is not a matter of social-economic status, education or intelligence. Our God desires to reveal himself to all people, no matter their race or gender, their intelligence, education or status in the community. All men alike can know and can receive revelation of the truth for Jesus has said, *"I am the way, the truth and the life"*. The writer of Hebrews says this about Jesus, *"...who, being the brightness of His glory and the express image of His person ..."*

For the religious, however, the blinders are still on for many when it comes to Jesus as their personal Lord and Savior.

We can know where to find Him.

To God it is all about relationship. God not only reveals himself as creator, the almighty one who is holy and just, but he also expresses Himself as Father. He watches over us as a shepherd watches over his sheep. He knows who are his and those who are not.

God is a spirit so we cannot see Him, but we only need to call upon Him and He will answer. This seems too simple-too easy. We feel we must make it more difficult. God is not a man that he should lie. Therefore we can find comfort when James writes in James 4:8, *"Draw near to God and He will draw near to you."*

WHAT DOES IT TAKE THEN TO FIND GOD? THE ANSWER IS SIMPLE; A HUMBLE HEART. GOD IS NOT FOUND IN NATURE, IN SOME MYSTICAL EXPERIENCE, OR IN A RELIGION. HE IS NOT FOUND HIDING AMONG HIS CREATION. HE IS NOT FOUND IN CARVED IMAGES OF WOOD OR STONE. HE IS FOUND, HOWEVER, WHEN WE HUMBLE OURSELVES AND CALL

OUT TO HIM. HE WILL REVEAL HIMSELF IN SUCH A WAY THAT WE WILL KNOW, THAT WE KNOW, THAT WE HAVE BEEN IN THE PRESENCE OF A LOVING, KIND AND ALMIGHTY GOD.

Question Two
What is the Nature of External Reality?

The Biblical Worldview recognizes, not only that there is a God, but also that this God created the universe and that he created it out of nothing. In Chapter 6 we saw the how and also the why God created the universe. There are some things that our God has not yet revealed, but knowledge about Himself and that which He has created are not part of that secret.

We marvel at the world we live in. It is orderly and everything in it has its right place. Like a multi-jeweled, highly sophisticated expensive watch, each part meshes perfectly with another to keep it going and going. Everything God created is GOOD.

All that God created was good, however, it all changed when man rebelled against God. God has said about Man, who he created in His image and after His likeness, in *Jer 17:9-10*, *"The heart is deceitful above all things, And desperately wicked; Who can know it? I, the Lord, search the heart?"*

The totality of our rebellion is seen in Romans 3:9-10 and 18. *"I have already charged that all men, both Jews and Greeks, are under the power of sin, as it is written: None is righteous, no not one; no one seeks for God...There is no fear of God before their eyes."*

In the beginning, Man was created good; but Adam's sin infected us all and we are at birth, unclean. This world system that we are now living in is under the curse of God and subject to the evil that prevails.

Question Three
What is a human being?

In Chapter 6 we discussed what Man is to God. We learned that it was all about a loving God's plan to have a family of sons. Therefore, He made Man in His own image, and after His own likeness. Man is a spirit that is capable of expression that can be

151

seen through his own Soul (will, emotions, and mind) and a body to carry out the dictates of his soul.

Man is created with a spirit and this "spirit" aspect of his life is God's connection to this world. God, by His Holy Spirit reaches out to Man from the spiritual realm to the physical realm to give wisdom, guidance, power, and to reveal His will. In the beginning, Man was without sin; therefore, there was unity and order in the universe.

The following Scriptures tell us that we are His people, and He is our God. These are His words to us. This is God reaching out to us, to bring us into His family.

- "But this is the covenant that I will make with the house of Israel after those days, says the Lord: I will put My law in their minds, and write it on their hearts; and I will be their God, and they shall be My people." Jer 31:33
- "They shall be My people, and I will be their God" Jer 32:38

God made Man to have fellowship with Him; Man (of his own free will) chose instead to rebel against God. In this rebellious state, Man opened the door for powerful forces of destruction to be unleashed upon the earth. He broke the connection.

Man, created in the image and likeness of God, was now a creature with a fallen nature, full of sinful desires whose final end was now an eternity separated from his creator. He had lost his relationship with a loving God to become a slave to the prince of this world; a liar, deceiver and who himself is a created being who would ultimately spend his eternity in the lake of fire.

Question Four
What Happens to a Person After Death?

In Genesis 3:22 God put Man out of the garden, because He would not, could not, allow a sinful man to be continually in his presence until he had repented , sought forgiveness and turned back to Him. Without repentance and obedience, there was no basis for a relationship.

For those that hold fast to a Biblical Worldview, death is not the end of the relationship and is not to be feared. Physical death actually allows this relationship to deepen, as the body will put off corruption and put on incorruption. The resurrection from the dead is a foundational belief for the Christian and without life after death, our faith in Jesus is worthless.

Hebrews 9:27 tells us that there is life after death for it states that, *"it is appointed for men to die once, but after this the judgment"*. There will be a judgment for the righteous and a judgment for the unrighteous. The righteous will go before the Judgment seat of Christ and the unrighteous will go before the Great White Throne for Judgment.

Chapters 6 and 7 describe the Kingdom of which we will be a part. This Kingdom will last for an eternity after our judgment.

Question Five
How is it Possible to Know Anything at All?

Realistic philosophy says, "The world is whatever it is, largely independent of what particular observers think about it – it is not a simple product of the human mind. For example, people used to think that the world was flat, but when they started thinking, it was round, we do not imagine that the earth itself changed shape. Its shape was unaffected by our ideas about it". In other words, it is what it is.

To those of the World—the world exists independently of their knowledge of it, but man's description of it depends on available knowledge and this knowledge must be built on previous knowledge. If one does not have previous knowledge, then he can go no further. An example; if one has not learned or come to know basic arithmetic; he cannot expect to come to know calculus.

The unbeliever's ideas of the world and of anything else are constructed by various ways of seeing—eyes, ears, heart—these are the methods that the World comes to 'know'. The unbeliever cannot step outside of these to see the world from another perspective, unlike the Believer.

Those that hold to a Biblical Worldview find that the Spirit of God opens up the door to another world, the spirit world that those without the Spirit of God cannot fathom. *1 Cor 2:9-1, But as it is written: "Eye has not seen, nor ear heard, Nor have entered into the heart of man The things which God has prepared for those who love*

Him." But God has revealed them to us through His Spirit. For the Spirit searches all things, yes, the deep things of God.

When we embrace a Biblical Worldview, our thinking is very different. We can know, not because of having prior knowledge upon which to build, but because our Prime Reality, who is unchanging and eternal and loving in character, chooses, above all else, to reveal all truth to us. His desire is to deliver us from the dominion of darkness, and to transfer us into the Kingdom of his beloved son. He reveals all things to us by his Spirit. This is why age, sex, education, culture or anything else does not enter into our ability to know God. (See John 16: 12-13, Jeremiah 33:3).

Question Six
What is Wrong or Right?

To a world that is getting more and more wicked, its only way to justify itself is to believe in the concept of *tolerance*. To the world there can be no moral absolutes -- no sin. Since we live in a world that is dominated by Satan, it is no wonder that so many of us give in to what is called Moral Relativism, 'What is right for one is not necessary right for another'. We do, however pass laws when there seems to be a group of people that are pushing the limit to satisfy "self". These are said to be, 'disregarding the rights of the majority'.

Societies have developed their own set of laws that govern the behavior of its people. The Apostle Paul has said it so aptly when he pointed out, *"For example, whenever non-Jews who don't have laws from God do by nature the things that Moses' Teachings contain, they are a law to themselves even though they don't have any laws from God. They show that some requirements found in Moses' Teachings are written in their hearts. Their consciences speak to them. Their thoughts accuse them on one occasion and defend them on another."* (Rom. 2:14-15, GW)

To those holding a Biblical Worldview—the Prime Reality (God) is not only love; He is also just. He is a God of justice. Justice has no value or meaning, if there is no right or wrong—good or evil. God is righteous and the scepter of his Kingdom is the scepter of righteousness, therefore God has given us principles to live by that will keep us within the boundaries of His Love. These

Principles are universal, timeless, and inarguable. Principles are, the guiding sense of the requirements and obligations of right conduct. We learned more about these Principles in Chapters 14 and 15.

Right and wrong is not based on decisions, but the consequences of those decisions are the result of choosing between Principles that govern our lives. These Principles are either correct or incorrect. Right and wrong will be revealed when we choose to follow right Principles or choose to follow something else.

Wisdom is ours if we choose to live by Godly Principles. God has given us this power to choose. It is our free will. The Godly Principles chosen will determine the effect of our decisions. God will view godly principles as righteous, while the decisions made by those of the world will result in their perishing.

Even among those that do not adhere to biblical truths, there is a law among them. There are things that they will not tolerate. Therefore, even they have their own sense of right and wrong.

Question Seven
What is the Meaning of History?

Early accounts of history were passed on by means of oral tradition and hand-written documents. These records of the past focused on human activity and became the field of research producing a continuous narrative and a systematic analysis of events that were of importance to the human race.

History is more than a record of events that have occurred around the world. It speaks of man's attempt to shape events, through his own intervention. Leaders, good and bad, have carved out a place in history as they have influenced others to take a certain course of action. Their worldview has led them to serve their own interests or to serve the general good of society.

If we have a Biblical Worldview, we can follow history and see how God -- the Prime Reality -- has executed a plan and has followed that plan throughout the course of history. He has given history a voice through the prophets, who have heralded His plan with great detail and exactness. History is proof that He is whom He said He is and is reason enough to give Him honor and glory.

History also proclaims God's mercy and grace, and vindicates God's proclamation of judgment upon evildoers. The fulfillment and realization of God's Word as proven by history; gives us hope and faith for the future.

The Nation of Israel was constantly reminded of their history and that God's hand was upon them to bring them out of Egypt and bring them into the Promised Land. Sadly the Nation of Israel did not heed or remember the purpose that God had for them.

A study of history can cause man to honor God or to seek his own way. He will see God's hand of provision and protection on His people or he will look at man's achievements and glory in them.

We take pictures to remind us of our history. We have pictures of grandparents, even great grandparents, hanging on walls. Pictures of children, from birth through grade school to college are proudly displayed. Our great vacations, wonderful moments such as marriage and graduations are there for all to see. They are our history.

What we do not display however, are our mistakes, wrong decisions, and failures. These too are part of our history. They are part of the Biblical history of God's covenant people also and are there for our instruction and learning.

Expanding our Worldview

Our two greatest needs are met with our Biblical Worldview; peace and freedom. We have peace within because the penalty for our rebellion has been paid and we are reconciled to our heavenly Father. We have freedom because we are free from the power of sin in our lives.

The Bible says, *"Therefore if the Son makes you free, you shall be free indeed"* and *"Peace I leave with you, My peace I give to you; not as the world gives do I give to you"*. Many have stopped at the cross; and proudly proclaim that the cross is the PLACE where one finds peace and freedom. Yes, it does start there but if we want to experience the Abundant Life that His Cross attains for us, we must follow Jesus, the Christ into the throne room. We must come to a realization that we are citizens of the kingdom – the Kingdom of God.

When we change how we perceive Jesus Christ, our Worldview will also change. We must be willing to let go of the things that have shaped our thinking and our belief system in the past and embrace something new that is based on revelation of the truth from God's Word.

A Kingdom Worldview begins with God the Father making a decision to extend His Kingdom to earth even before it or anything else existed, including Man. God creates the earth and everything humans need to maintain life, then at last, He creates Man. He creates man in His image and His likeness and gives him dominion over all that He had created in order that he may govern on His behalf.

God's connection with man is through His Spirit and Man's spirit. Man is to mature in his relationship with His Creator in order to fulfill his assignment as ruler of the new kingdom. He is to fill the earth with his offspring and instill the culture of the Kingdom into all aspects of Kingdom life. The culture that develops in the extended kingdom is to duplicate that of the Kingdom of Heaven. The family unit is to be a miniature picture of the Kingdom of God here on earth. Therefore, as more families are established, the Kingdom of God is extended throughout the Earth. Eventually the Earth is covered with the glory of the Lord as the Kingdom of God is spread in every corner of our globe.

Our ability to appreciate a Kingdom Worldview will be determined by the way we "see" God. When we have an Encounter with God, it is our view of God that will birth the faith that will then forge our experience. As an example, if we only see God as Savior our faith will be strong in that area but weak in other areas, such as Healer. However, if we see God as King, our faith will allow us to experience God in all areas that His names express because this title encompasses all the others.

Following on page 159 are 42 different names that the Bible uses to describe our God. There are many more and I encourage you to add to this list. Read over these names and use your imagination to wrap your arms around our most amazing God who can meet your every need. I have purposely left some of the list to encourage you to search your Bible and take out paper and pen.

We know that there is no earthly place we can be free from the evils of this world's culture. This is so because the heart of Man is deceitfully wicked and is distinguish by, *"fornication, impurity, licentiousness, idolatry, sorcery, enmity, strife, jealousy, anger, selfishness, dissension, party spirit, envy, drunkenness, carousing, and the like."* (Gal 5:19-21). Nevertheless, we can be free just the same. We can be free because the only place that offers the peace and freedom that we seek is the Kingdom of God and it is within us.

The Kingdom of God is not a physical place, but it is the governmental rule of God in our heart. The rule of God is over its citizens who are a community of like-minded people. Collectively it is the hearts of the citizens that allow them live out the Sermon on the Mount and individually express the fruit of the Spirit of God: love, peace, joy, patience, kindness, goodness, gentleness and faithfulness. (Gal. 5:22).

Together with the character of its citizens and the power of the King, a Kingdom Worldview distinguishes itself from other Worldviews. It is with such a worldview that the Father can find fulfillment of His Grand Plan for mankind.

---

[1] James Sire, The Universe Next Door, page 17
[2] Professor Henry Calderwood, Handbook of Moral Philosophy, page 188 #7

Names of God

A Sure Foundation - Isa. 28:16

Our Guide - Ps. 48:14

My Advocate – Job 16:19

A Great High Priest - Heb. 4:14

Bread of Life - John 6:35

My Confidence - Ps. Ps. 71:5

Defender of widows – Ps. 68:5

Faithful and True – Rev. 19:11

A Consuming Fire Deut. 4:24

My Friend – Job 16:20

God of all comfort – 2Cor. 1:3

God who saves me – Ps. 51:14

Head of the Church – Eph. 5:23

My Hiding Place – Ps. 32:7

Holy among you – Hos. 11:9

Righteous Judge – 2 Tim. 4:8

Our leader – 2 Chron. 13:12

Light of life – John 8:12

The Most Holy – Dan. 9:24

Good Teacher – Mark 10:17

My Support – 2 Sam. 22:19

God Who avenges me - Ps. 18:4

Your Life – Col. 3:4

Sovereign Lord – Luke 2:29

Our Help - Ps. 33:20

Comforter in sorrow - Jer. 8:18

Wonderful Counselor - Isa. 9:6

My Strong Deliver - Ps. 140:7

Our Father Isa. - 64:8

God Almighty - Gen. 17:15

My Redeemer – Ps. 19:14

King of Kings – 1 Tim. 6:15

Jealous – Ex. 34:14

Prince of Peace – Isa. 9:6

Refuge and strength – Ps. 46:1

My Hope - Ps. 71:5

My Stronghold – Ps. 18:2

My Salvation – Ex. 15:2

My Savior – Ps. 42

Our Peace – Eph. 2:14

Mediator – 1 Tim. 2:15

Lord of Lords – 1 Tim. 6:15

Chapter Nineteen

Response to Joni E. Tada

Healing Calmly Considered

On pages 15-16, we mentioned several assertions made by Joni regarding her healing and that of others. Because she has given herself to the Lord, He has promoted her to a position of influence. That position however, does not make her a spokesperson for God on the subject of healing. Unfortunately, her influence will keep many in their bed of affliction instead of praising God for His love and power. Allow me to address each one:

"Does that mean "rise & walk" miracles are for everyone?" The real question is, is there a need for a healing or a need for a miracle. Sickness and disease are the result of the rebellion in the Garden of Eden. Broken vertebrae, because of a fall, are something entirely different. In regards to sickness, faith in the finished work of Christ's atonement is needed. In regards to a broken vertebra, faith in miracles for today must be present. To be made whole faith, along with a Rhema word, is required and is needed for both. A Rhema word is a word from God spoken directly to you and results in faith being released.

"The Bible doesn't teach it and experience doesn't support it." When a person does not receive what they pray for, they don't want to blame the lack of results on their lack of faith so they come up with another reason for defeat. This is hard to swallow but others can take just the opposite position and say the Bible does teach it and millions of people that were sick are now well.

Here is the point: We must not engage in any speculation as to why they are not healed. This is a very sensitive area and we do not want to discourage faith but to encourage faith in God.

However, let me address this issue. Just because people say they believe does not mean that, they have faith. Faith is the answer to everything. Faith comes from revelation not by study itself. Faith is given as a result of seeking God, not by trying to find the answer from pages in a book, even if it's the Bible.

Here is a bigger point: What we find in the church community today are people trying to persuade others to their point of view. They want to win an argument and thereby, feel superior about their knowledge of the Bible. "KINGDOM CONNECTIONS" does not try to win any argument but present truth that brings about wholeness to spirit, soul and body.

"There are two conditions for answered prayer". There are at least five conditions for answered prayer; not just the two that Joni mentioned.

- Abide in Jesus – (John 15:7-8)
- Pray in accordance with the will of God – (1 John 5:14-45)
- Pray in the name of Jesus – (John 16:23)
- Ask in prayer, believing – (Matt. 21:22)
- Abide in the Word – (John 15:7)

Joni has overlooked the last three conditions.

"... and that our requests be in line with God's will. Because God hasn't chosen to reveal every detail of his will to Christians, then we must leave our requests in His hands". The problem is God has commanded us to pray according to the will of God. How can we pray according to the will of God and not know the will of God. The scripture says that, *"if we ask anything according to His will, he hears us: and if we know that he hears us, whatsoever we ask, we know that we have the petitions that we asked of Him".*

How could we trust God for anything if He doesn't let us know His will? Is this how you would treat your children, your loved ones? Do you keep them guessing as to what your will is? God does reveal his will to us by His Spirit. If we don't develop our fellowship with the Holy Spirit and sharpen our listening skills in order to hear His voice and promptings, we will come to our own conclusions. Joni's Worldview embraces Predeterminism.

"He will glorify Himself by our suffering." There is nowhere in the Bible where God is glorified by the suffering of mankind. In fact, just the opposite is the case. It was when the sick were

healed and the blind given back their sight that God was glorified. *"'Woman, you are loosed from your infirmity.' And He laid His hands on her, and immediately she was made straight, and* **glorified God***."* (Luke 13:12-13). *"And one of them, when he saw that he was healed, returned, and with a loud voice* **glorified God***,* Luke 17:15-16, emphasis mine.

Now, if she means that through our suffering we are changed, as she was by devoting her life to God and learning to live with her situation, then is God glorified? Yes, others will see God at work within us but let us not say that God is limiting his glory because that is His Will.

To develop a good attitude toward her paralysis is not a miracle as she said. It is commendable, honorable, courageous, it is worthy of praise; but it is not a miracle. Hundreds of thousands of Christians around the world have fallen to a similar fate as Joni. These people, not having the same support system, money, and love from family and medical treatment have not been as victorious as she has. These have succumbed to bitterness, despair and have become burdensome to others instead of being productive in the Kingdom of God. Is this the work then of a sovereign God?

We are not called to be spiritual watchdogs or commentators on the faith or lack of faith regarding other believers. Overcomers are called to present truths that WORK and change people's lives, God is not interested in our ability to win a theological argument; what He is interested in is for His people to trust Him and for us to take back what Satan has stolen. The truth will set others and ourselves FREE!

A Simple Presentation of the

The Gospel of the Kingdom of God

D o you know why you were created? Do you know what purpose the Creator has in your being born? The answer to these questions will solve all the other questions that you have about life and the pain, sorrow, and tragedies that we suffer.

The answer is not difficult, it is plain and simple. God, the creator of all things, spiritual and physical, desired to share His life with others who would share His love. Being King and having dominion over all His Creation is part of His life. Just as an earthly father wants to pass on to his children his business, God wanted to pass on to those who would become His children, His family business - the rule over a Kingdom.

In order to accomplish this purpose, God extended His Kingdom from the spiritual realm to the physical. He created the heavens and the earth and then created Man (Adam and Eve) and told them to *"be fruitful, multiply, fill the earth, subdue it and have dominion"*.

Because Man was created in the image and the likeness of God he was able to fulfill this command. What that simple means is that he was given the character, the knowledge and the ability to do carry out his role as God's ruling agent upon the earth. His ability to rule is tied to the relationship that he enjoyed with an almighty God.

What happened next is the beginning of all the sorrow, pain, suffering and tragedies upon the earth. Adam and Eve allowed Satan, an angel whose pride caused him to rebel against God, to use a snake to deceive them into thinking that they could disobey God's direct command without any consequences.

However, as soon as they rebelled, God barred them from His direct presence and mankind came under the control of the new ruler of the earth, Satan. What they immediately realized was, not only did they lose dominion of the kingdom but they also lost their intimate relationship with God, their creator. Of equal consequence of their rebellion was that now all their descendants would inherit the same rebellious and corrupt nature.

The Good News

Because sin is not just some wrong done by man but is inherent in his character, death is the only justice accepted. A natural parallel to this is; when a dog goes into a hen house and eats the hens and the eggs, the dog must be killed. He is killed, not because of the act of what he did, but because what he did has become part of his nature and he will kill again and again. The same can be said when a bear or a tiger kill a human.

Because we all have sinned, someone human like us, but without sin, had to pay the penalty in order for justice to be satisfied. The only one who fit that description was Jesus, therefore it was Jesus who went to the cross and took upon himself the sin of all mankind, past and future. He paid the penalty due to the sinful nature, for all mankind, just as if it was his own.

Jesus, God's Word made visible in the flesh, came to reclaim His Father's Kingdom and to redeem Man from the control of Satan. Sin had separated Man from God therefore Jesus came to pay the penalty that would satisfy the justice of God and restore the relationship.

Since death is the only Justice accepted by a Holy and Righteous God, the only solution that would make it possible for God to fulfill His original purpose for Man was to give him a new heart. This God does when we confess to having a sinful nature and believe by faith in this act of love by Jesus that makes possible for each of us to find freedom from the guilt of our own individual, personal sin.

By the sacrificing of his body and the shedding of his blood, Jesus made it possible for you and for me to be reconciled to our creator and become children in the family of God. Our faith in Jesus as our Savior made it possible for us to be "born again". And as "born again" people we can now enter the Kingdom of God.

The most profound statement Jesus made was when He was asked by the Pharisees when the kingdom of God would come. He said, *"God's kingdom is coming but not in the way that you will be able to see it with your eyes. People will not say, 'look, here it is!' or 'there it is!' because God's kingdom is within you."* NCV

Jesus is not only the Savior from the penalty of our sinful nature but He is now the King over our new heart. We do not need to go another place to find peace and freedom because the Kingdom is within us. Jesus sets up His rule in our hearts.

The Good News of the Kingdom is not limited to our being reconciled to our creator. We are not just "in" the Kingdom; we are made citizens of the Kingdom. As citizens of the Kingdom of God we have certain rights and responsibilities. There are benefits to living under the government of the one who has ALL authority and power.

The first benefit is; should we die before Jesus returns for His Church, we have the assurance that our spirit and soul will be with our King in Heaven. The second benefit is that while we are here on earth, we have access to the healing and delivering power of our God. The third benefit is that He crowns us with loving-kindness and tender mercies. God's Grand Plan for us, however, is for us to rule and reign with Christ over a new earth for an eternity.

Our responsibility is to live as loyal and faithful citizens of the Kingdom. We are to bring glory to our King by giving Him honor and living righteously, for His Kingdom is a kingdom based on Righteousness and Justice. We are to express the culture of the Kingdom for others to see and invite them into the kingdom.

Asking for a Response

The benefit of entering the Kingdom of God is not that you go to another place (Heaven) when you die but that you enter into a relationship with the King. It is instantaneous and it is from this relationship that your faith grows and causes you to know that you are entitled to the benefits of citizenship in the Kingdom. These benefits are not for the future but for the today.

The Gospel of the Kingdom of God

Are you longing for a relationship with the King of the Kingdom that will last for an eternity?

The Bible tells us that, "*...Don't fool yourselves. Those who indulge in sexual sin, or who worship idols, or commit adultery, or are male prostitutes, or practice homosexuality, or are thieves, or greedy people, or drunkards, or are abusive, or cheat people—none of these will inherit the Kingdom of God*" I Cor 6: 9-10

Jesus said, "*Repent, for the kingdom of God is at hand*". Repent means to change your thinking. Whether you recognize it or not, what you have thought all along, is that you would never be held accountable for your lying, sealing, or whatever. Because God calls that behavior "sin" (and we all have sinned) we will be held accountable.

But like the dog that killed the hens, it is not your actions but the sin found in your heart, your character that is the problem. That is why Jesus told the religious Jewish Priest, "*Unless you are Born Again, you cannot enter the Kingdom of God*". The penalty is severe; it is eternal separation from your Creator. Your only hope is to confess your sin and throw yourself on the mercy of a loving Almighty God. You must be 'born again'.

He loves you and holds out His hand to you and invites you to enter His kingdom. Jesus is not only the King but is also the door into the Kingdom.

It is only your act of faith in Christ Jesus that will give you the peace within that comes from being forgiven and the freedom not to be overcome by the chaos in this world. Yes, it is your faith in His sinless life, His death upon the cross-taking your sin upon Himself, His resurrection from the dead and His ascension to His throne in Heaven that will allow you to stand without shame before Almighty God. It is your Faith that will cause God to give you a new Heart and welcome you into the Kingdom

He is waiting for your answer!

Scriptures for the presentation are available on our website

www.kingdomfaithconnection.com

About the Author

Robert Farrier

Robert Farrier, founder of Kingdom Connections, travels internationally proclaiming the gospel of the Kingdom and awakening God's people to the wonder of Living in the Kingdom.

He is a product of the Charismatic movement and since that time he has held strong to the belief that the Word of God is the standard by which all things are to be judged. He has remembered a saying he learned from his pastor long ago, "If you guide your life by just the Word you will dry up. If you guide your life by just the Spirit you will blow up. If you allow the Spirit to guide your life by the Word, you will grow up." Therefore, he has held to a balance of the Word and the Spirit.

Robert graduated from Southeastern University in 1979. He went on pastor in Vermont and New York. Later, as Director of Education in a large Church in Upstate New York, Robert's interests in mentoring the saints in the fulfilling of God's Grand Plan began to emerge.

In the last 20 years Robert has traveled overseas to the underdeveloped nations holding Pastor Conferences and preaching on the streets to awaken a vision of the Kingdom of God. He shares the principles that he learned in his daily walk with the Lord regarding the leading of the Spirit that produces lasting results. Robert continues his ministry today to the nations of the world with an emphasis in Haiti.

The revelation of the principles of Transformation and Empowerment are now incorporated in the teaching and preaching ministry of Kingdom Connections, Inc, a non-profit ministry. For several years Robert has been teaching the material that is now found in two of his books, *"BORN TO RULE"* and *"A KNIGDOM WHICH CANNOT BE SHAKEN"*.

Robert draws on his 38 years of walking with the Lord, his experience as a Pastor, Missionary/Evangelist, and Teacher. He is available for weekend Seminars and Pastor's Conferences.

Bob and his wife, Bea, of 49 years live in Dania Beach, FL.

You can contact Robert at
bob@kingdomfaithconnection.com

Please check out the Kingdom Connections website:
www.kingdomfaithconnection.com